To Tom & Diane
Hope you enjoy the book
Best wishes!
"Desser"

# A COACH'S WORLD

# A COACH'S WORLD

## RICHARD "DIGGER" PHELPS
### AND LARRY KEITH

THOMAS Y. CROWELL COMPANY
NEW YORK   ESTABLISHED *1834*

Portions of this work were adapted from a *Sports Illustrated* article entitled "The End of a Week That Never Was," written by Larry Keith for that magazine.

Photographs by Rich Clarkson for *Sports Illustrated,* © Time, Inc., except where otherwise credited.

Manufactured in the United States of America

Library of Congress Cataloging in Publication Data

Phelps, Richard.
    A coach's world.

    1. Phelps, Richard.  2. Basketball.  3. Basketball coaching.  4. Notre Dame, Ind.  University—Basketball.  I.  Keith, Larry, joint author.  II. Title.
GV884.P45A33        796.32′3′0924 [B]        74–17182
ISBN 0–690–00560–1

                1   2   3   4   5   6   7   8   9   10

*To Terry, Carolyn,
and Our Parents*

# ACKNOWLEDGMENTS

The authors would like to thank the players and assistant coaches of the University of Notre Dame basketball team, whose cooperation made this book possible. Thanks also to Roger Valdiserri and Bob Best, for opening the files and resources of the Notre Dame Sports Information Office; to Dottie Van Paris of the Notre Dame Basketball Office, for transcribing hours of tapes; and to Carolyn Keith of *Sports Illustrated*, for photographic research and editorial assistance.

DIGGER PHELPS
*South Bend, Indiana*

LARRY KEITH
*New York, New York*

# A COACH'S WORLD

## SATURDAY, OCTOBER 30, 1965

The head basketball coach at St. Gabriel's High School in Hazleton, Pennsylvania, mails a letter to the head football coach at the University of Notre Dame in South Bend, Indiana. "Knowing you have little time to waste," Dick Phelps writes to Ara Parseghian, "I don't expect you to answer in the near future, but I would appreciate a short reply after the season, if your busy schedule permits. Eventually I'd like to coach on the college level. My big dream is to coach basketball at Notre Dame. I love the essence that makes Notre Dame what it is . . . someday I hope that I might be a part of that program." Just a year ago, while Parseghian was regilding the Golden Dome by winning nine of ten games and the MacArthur Bowl in his first season with the Irish, Phelps, in his first season anywhere, was leading Junior High School 4 of Trenton, New Jersey, to a 2–6 record. Now, at twenty-four, upwardly mobile and soon to be a father, Phelps is not without his visions.

## TUESDAY, MAY 4, 1971

Phelps is sitting in his tiny basement office on the Bronx, New York, campus of Fordham University, awaiting a phone call that is six years and thirty minutes overdue. The six years have been prosperous ones; the Pennsylvania Class C high school championship, four outstanding freshmen teams while an assistant coach at the University of Pennsylvania, and a 26–3 season as head coach at Fordham. The last thirty minutes have been agonizing. When the phone finally rings Phelps tries very hard to sound relaxed as he answers, "Hello?" In return he expects to hear a voice summoning him to Notre Dame. Only the call isn't from the school. It is a friend wanting to hear the good news. "No, not yet," Phelps says hurriedly, "they're a half hour late and they may be trying to call now." A few minutes later the phone rings again. It is the call for which he has been waiting a long, long time.

## SATURDAY, OCTOBER 16, 1971

One day after his first practice session, the new Irish basketball coach is standing in the press box of Notre Dame Stadium, awaiting the start of a football game against North Carolina. It is a crisp, clear day, an Indiana autumn at its best. While players and fans listen to the brassy strains of the national anthem, Phelps leans over and whispers to a friend, "This is it, this is what I always wanted. I can hardly believe it. I think I'm going to cry."

*Notre Dame* . . . no other school so intrigues public curiosity or inspires such wide-ranging emotional response. Nowhere else is identification with athletic prosperity so easily made. Its heroes are legendary, its high moments incalculable.

The circumstances that brought Digger Phelps to this 1,250-acre campus on the northern border of Indiana reflect the inner workings, and unravel some of the enigmas, that make Notre Dame what it is. No one takes the mythos of Irish athletics quite so seriously as the people who give intercollegiate sports at Notre Dame their direction and point of view. Both Fr. Edmund P. Joyce, chairman of the Faculty Board in Control of Athletics, and Edward (Moose) Krause, athletic director, attended the school in the 1930's. Each left the womb for a few years, only to return in the 1940's, first Krause to coach the basketball team and then Joyce to be ordained into the priesthood. They assumed their present positions within a few years of each other. Krause, four years older, and an All-American in both football and basketball, became athletic director in 1949; Fr. Joyce was appointed executive vice president in 1952. For them the old echoes did not need to be awakened; they were never asleep.

Phelps' campaign to coach at Notre Dame began with his letter to Ara Parseghian in 1965. Four years later, secure in his reputation as an outstanding assistant coach, he gained an introduction to Krause through Johnny Druze, a mutual acquaintance. Druze, one of Fordham's famous Seven Blocks of Granite in the 1930's, was a long-time friend and former coaching associate of Krause. His daughter had recently married a friend of Digger's. For Phelps, the ties were close enough.

"Johnny gave me a call," Krause says, "and told me he knew a young man who was just the kind of coach we should have at Notre Dame. Johnny had coached here himself and he knew what our philosophy was. I said I would meet Phelps and, frankly, I enjoyed him.

"Whenever he was in the South Bend area we would have

lunch. I quizzed him about different things because I wondered what a young lad like him thought. The more he talked, the more I became impressed. I told him that if anything did open up here in the next year or two we might have something for him."

From the moment of their first meeting Phelps measured every step in his career by its relevance to an eventual job at Notre Dame. He was not unhappy working under Dick Harter at Pennsylvania; in fact, he refused higher-paying assistant's positions offered by three schools in the prestigious Atlantic Coast Conference: Maryland, Duke, and Virginia. "I wouldn't have left Penn for a similar job at any place except Notre Dame," he says. But he did seek the head position at Seton Hall because "I thought by doing well at another Catholic school it would help me get to Notre Dame." However, he was barely considered.

Phelps did not realize that he was already the leading candidate to succeed the controversial, though successful, Johnny Dee. "I might not have minded the gamble of hiring an assistant if the opportunity had come," says Krause. "What Phelps did at Fordham the year after we met only verified what I first thought about him."

Phelps' conduit to Fordham once again had been Druze, who arranged an interview for him with Athletic Director Pete Carlesimo. Rejected elsewhere, Phelps was hired at Fordham, where his sudden success included a stunning 94–88 upset of Notre Dame.

The Fordham loss made Dee all the more unpopular with the Irish athletic hierarchy. "We had no business losing to Fordham that year," Fr. Joyce says. "That team looked like it should have won the national championship, but it was too disorganized." Fr. Joyce was frustrated by a Dee record whose big wins—such as the victory over UCLA—only made the defeats more disappointing.

Krause's objections to the coach were also personal; it was

no secret the two did not get along. "Dee wanted to be a big success and use Notre Dame as the stepping stone," Krause says.

The situation climaxed with Dee's resignation in May 1971. "Johnny was planning to stay only one more year anyway," says Fr. Joyce, "but I suggested this might be the best time for him to leave." Meanwhile, Phelps had become a strong candidate to replace Harter, who had left Penn for Oregon. But, for once, the timing was perfect. "Digger called almost immediately to say he was still interested in Notre Dame," says Krause. "Actually, I wasn't interested in interviewing anybody else."

Even with the support of Krause, Phelps could not be hired without the final approval of Fr. Joyce and the Faculty Board. "We run a pretty tight ship," he says. "The big decisions are made here."

Phelps' only competition was generated by one of Dee's assistants, Gene Sullivan, who won the endorsement of influential alumni and other coaches in the athletic department, including Parseghian. (Ara had long forgotten that hopeful letter from a young Pennsylvania high school coach.) Fr. Joyce was not swayed. He sought a coach not unlike his vision of Parseghian, a man of proven talents, inspirational qualities, and unquestioned honesty. He did not want outside pressure, a continuation of the Dee regime, or a man without collegiate head coaching experience. Of the latter point he says, "We had been burned with Terry Brennan [Frank Leahy's twenty-five-year-old successor in 1954] and I didn't want that to happen again."

Finally, Fr. Joyce imposed one other condition. He wanted a winner. "There has always been an intense desire to excel here," he says, "because we are a closely knit community. Being predominantly male gives us something of a Spartan atmosphere from which athletics is a normal outgrowth. This was the fertile ground that enabled Rockne's genius for leadership and motivation to flower. We are pleased it has developed this way."

This tradition is not without its influence on the modern Notre Dame coach. "We're not ruthless, but we are sort of spoiled about winning," Fr. Joyce admits. "Winning and losing will always take care of itself here. When a coach doesn't do well right away, there may be subtle pressure on him to succeed, but it's not anything that could cost him his job as long as he is living within the program. We will always give a coach what it takes to get the job done, because we are striving to be nationally competitive and we are in the enviable position of not having to scrimp. But we're not willing to pay an improper price for success. We want to be as good as we can without sacrificing our principles."

Fr. Joyce believes that Notre Dame's athletic and academic reputation is such that "we ought to be able to get pretty good athletes." He believes that the twin-domed $8.6-million Athletic and Convocation Center that was completed in 1968 is best utilized when there is a winning team on the floor and something close to 11,345 people in the stands.

So, in May 1971, he agreed with his athletic director that young Digger Phelps met Notre Dame's criteria. "We wanted somebody who would believe in the emotional side of our campus," said Krause, "the way Rockne and Leahy did."

In that respect, certainly, Digger Phelps was their man.

## MONDAY, OCTOBER 15, 1973

Day One and the Fighting Irish of the University of Notre Dame, seven weeks away from their opening game against Valparaiso on December 1, are undefeated and undeterred.

Also a little unprepared for what they find when they walk out onto the hard, polished wood of the Athletic and Convocation Center basketball floor. Four girls are among the students answering Digger Phelps' annual invitation for open tryouts on the first day of practice.

Only two years ago one of them, perhaps the diminutive black girl who claims to be an all-stater from Georgia, might have had a chance. But today, for the first time in his three years at Notre Dame, Phelps has an encouraging blend of veteran and youthful talent. All five starters have returned from last year's National Invitational Tournament team: center John Shumate, forwards Gary Novak and Peter Crotty, guards Gary Brokaw and Dwight Clay. Furthermore, Phelps and his two assistants, Dick DiBiaso, thirty-two, and Frank McLaughlin, twenty-six, have recruited six freshmen whose prospects can be judged promising to spectacular. They include forwards Adrian Dantley and Bill Paterno; guards Ray Martin, Bill Drew, and Dave Kuzmicz; and center Toby Knight. Somewhere in that collection of strong, agile bodies is the proper combination of five players which will comprise this year's starting team.

In the vernacular of his fellow coaches, Digger Phelps has "built a program," not an unexpected achievement, but it did come sooner than almost anybody anticipated. Only two years ago a ragtag assortment of Notre Dame players showed up for every one of twenty-six games, and won all but twenty of them. In his very first season Phelps had managed the second-worst record in the school's history. The severe plunge following four consecutive twenty-or-more-game winners under Johnny Dee was not wholly unexpected, however. There was only one letterman on the entire squad. Two of the players were loaners from Parseghian's football team, brothers Willie and Mike Townsend. Two more were, in fact, nonscholarship walk-ons who emerged from an open tryout just like today's.

In comparison, last year had been a major triumph, as the

young Irish lineup of four sophomores and the junior Novak won twelve of its last fourteen games to finish 15–11 and capture an NIT bid. The strongest factor in the deliberations of the selection committee, however, was the Notre Dame alumni who would likely follow the Irish into Madison Square Garden. But once invited, the team proved its worthiness. Playing their first game on St. Patrick's Day, the Irish upset Southern California 69–65. Three days later Louisville fell 79–71, and then North Carolina, the NIT favorite, went down 78–71. Suddenly, there was Notre Dame in the nationally televised finals of the nation's oldest postseason tournament, paired against Virginia Tech, a Southern independent with a fine 25–5 record. The Irish lost the game 92–91 in overtime but won national stature nonetheless. Notre Dame, it seemed, had been raised from the dead by an undertaker's son called Digger.

## TUESDAY, OCTOBER 16

Today Phelps begins the serious business of evaluating talents, teaching strategy, and shaping discipline. The players have been practicing their own preliminary rite since the first week they arrived on campus. In pickup games of three-on-three or four-on-four they have been staking out their territory, proving their individual merit. Shumate's bruising power, Brokaw's graceful finesse, and Clay's long-armed quickness are by now very familiar. So, in fact, are the skills of all the players. There is not one on the roster of eighteen who did not come to Notre Dame with a creditable dossier of high school accomplishments. Chris Stevens, for instance, captained his team at St. John's Academy in Washington, D.C. But four years later Hawk is better known for his good humor, his campus radio show, and his participation in school politics than his basketball ability. Not surprisingly, he was irritated in those pickup games by Dantley, the celebrated high school All-America from his home town. Stevens felt Dantley did not pass the ball enough. For himself, the proud Dantley sought only to justify the publicity and attention that followed him to Notre Dame.

Throughout this first afternoon's practice Phelps is typically demanding, critical, sarcastic. The players understand and accept this, or at least the upperclassmen do, because they respect his ability to teach the game and motivate them to their best performances. "That's his way, that's how he makes his point," says Dwight Clay. "His hollering doesn't bother me." There is also the knowledge that he is not always so harsh, that his concern for them exceeds their importance as basketball players and that, very often, he can be a pretty good guy. And, of course, there is one other reason—they really don't have a choice. "Last year," says John Shumate, the team's best and most outspoken player, "some of the guys didn't understand how Digger could be so different on and off the court. But he finally made us believe that if we did things his way we could win. He kept telling us we could go to the NIT and by the time we got there we had started believing him."

The better side of Phelps' nature only becomes apparent midway through practice when his blonde, English-born wife Terry walks into the arena with their three children: Karen, eight on November 22, Rick, six, and Jennifer, four. Phelps smiles, waves, and stops practice long enough to lower the rebounding machine for Rick to shoot at.

* * *

During the basketball season I'm not always the easiest person to be around. When a player isn't concentrating or playing within his capability, I get on him. I don't like unnecessary distractions, either. If this book becomes one, I'll forget the book.

I'm an emotional person. The people who know me and appreciate what I'm trying to do, accept this as part of my coaching style on the court and my personality off it. Of course, I'm no different from a lot of other coaches and I no longer get as uptight as I once did. Certainly I'm not as intense as Bobby Knight at Indiana, but he was the one coaching in the final four at St. Louis last year, not me. And I'll let you in on a little secret: during the football season Ara's assistant coaches walk the ACC halls pretty softly. Not because he is any sort of ogre, but because he has a terribly difficult job and they appreciate it.

Terry, Frank, and Dick know that occasionally the best thing to say to me is absolutely nothing. They can read my ups and downs. Other times I might be as open and relaxed as anybody.

My personality around the players is something different. Sometimes I only want them to *think* I'm angry. I can turn the sugar on and off depending, not on how I feel, but on how I want *them* to feel. I don't know what is more difficult, actually, trying to convince a team you are scared to death of an opponent when you know you should win by thirty points, or trying to appear very loose and confident when you believe the world is about to fall down around you.

I don't want to sound as if I am being dishonest with anyone; if anything I'm being dishonest with myself. What I'm really talking about is motivating a player to his best performance in a way that suits my personality as his coach. I can't be eighteen different coaches for eighteen different players. They have to have faith in the goals we're trying to accomplish. They must concentrate, work hard, and accept the discipline I think is necessary.

I'm not running a democracy, I'm running a basketball team. If the players and assistants share my goals and believe in the way I want to do things, I think we will be successful.

## WEDNESDAY, OCTOBER 17

The undergraduate and graduate business administration degrees Phelps earned at Rider College in Trenton are given practical application at Notre Dame. It is the unseen responsibilities of a coach which demand most of his time, the administrative and organizational duties not unlike those of any executive who oversees a business that will gross $200,000 in four months of operation. Like every head coach at Notre Dame, Phelps falls third in the athletic chain of command, behind Fr. Joyce and Krause. But in the day-to-day affairs he has total authority to run his own program. He is answerable to his superiors—and conscious of their guidelines—but he seldom sees or hears from them. Symbolically, Phelps is as remote from them in distance as he is in daily responsibility. Fr. Joyce's office is in the Administration Building, the ninety-four-year-old "Golden Dome." Krause is on the second floor of the Athletic and Convocation Center, located on Juniper Road directly across from the football stadium on the eastern reach of the campus.

The basketball offices are on the ground floor of the ACC, sharing a corridor with the football staff's. Phelps' comfortable, blue-carpeted, wood-paneled corner office is flanked on either side by his two assistants'. They have the services of one full-time secretary, Mrs. Dottie Van Paris, and a part-time student.

The flow of paperwork and correspondence is enormous, and even the frothiest piece of mail is answered. One of the letters Phelps finds on his desk when he arrives at nine o'clock this morning is from Jim Hallihan, an assistant coach at Virginia Tech. It is a friendly note, informing Phelps that Hallihan enjoyed their meeting at a recent clinic in Washington. Enclosed is a matchbook imprinted "Notre Dame NIT Losers." The jibe is well taken.

In Notre Dame's dressing room, an accommodating facility with blue carpets, yellow walls, and private lockers and stools for each of the players, there are two signs on display. One of them asks "Greensboro?", a pointed reminder of this season's NCAA tournament site. The other says "Virginia Tech." Phelps is keen on the impact of such psychological ploys. "One tells the players what we are after," he explains, "and the other keeps us humble while we're getting there."

Dictation done, Phelps calls in DiBiaso and McLaughlin for their regular morning meeting. It is in this sixty-to-ninety minute session that the major and minor decisions of running a big-time college program are discussed. At one point DiBiaso says, "We've got to make clear to the guys that it's going to be both team offense and team defense this year and if they don't go along, we're going to substitute because we have the depth and talent to do it."

Already, Phelps and his staff are thinking positively about the coming season.

\*   \*   \*

I thought we were among the Top 20 teams in the country last year. I know the final polls did not include us but, based on our play in the second half of the season and on through the NIT, we deserved more recognition than we received. So, obviously, I feel optimistic about our prospects for this year. Not only do we have fine players returning but we've also added some outstanding freshmen.

We have one goal this season, to win enough games to get an NCAA bid. There will be nine at-large berths given out on February 28 by the tournament selection committee and I hope we are in a position to receive one. I think eighteen to twenty victories in our twenty-six-game schedule should be enough. That means we must win at least thirteen of our fifteen home games and about six of our eleven road games. It will not be easy, but we should be able to do it. In my opinion, we're one of the Top 10 teams in the country.

As I look at our schedule, it is obvious we face some very tough opponents. We are the only team outside the Pacific-8 playing UCLA twice. Indiana, Kentucky, Marquette, and South Carolina were all in the Top 20 last year and will be tough again this season.

Some of our other games will be difficult, if only because they are away from home. I'm very concerned about our four December road games against Big Ten opponents Ohio State, Northwestern, Indiana, and Michigan State. I haven't always liked the officiating on previous Big Ten trips—but I guess you never do when you lose. Let's just say I'm anxious to see what happens. Playing at Kansas should also be tough because they will be better after an off year. The best thing about our game at Dayton is that we go there after the bids have been offered. Then there are my two homecoming games, at the Palestra in Philadelphia against LaSalle and at Madison Square Garden in New York against Fordham.

I know there are some sure wins on our schedule because I tried, as does every coach, to make it that way. There are also some games which a lot of people will expect us to lose. But most of them could go either way and they are the ones we must win to get a bid. If you'd guarantee me a 20–6 record and an invitation to the Mideast Regional right now, I'd take it. To do that we'd have to beat some very good basketball teams.

## THURSDAY, OCTOBER 18

Competition for the gold practice-jersey worn by members of the first team is beginning to build, though the "Iron Five" of last year remains intact. Crotty and Novak, the 6′ 8″ and 6′ 7″ forwards, are acutely aware of the threat brought by brash newcomers Dantley and Paterno. Both speak warily of the "increased competition for positions" and the need for "maximum individual effort." Privately, they fear that their starting positions are in danger.

Crotty feels especially vulnerable. An outstanding career at St. Agnes Cathedral High School in Rockville Centre, New York, made him highly sought after. Eventually he decided to stay in the New York area and play under the young, energetic coach at Fordham, Digger Phelps. "I got very close to Digger and the Fordham players while I was being recruited," Crotty recalls. Peter possesses a friendly smile and, like Shumate, responds to questions willingly. "I'd go up to the campus a lot on my own. I couldn't wait for school to start so I'd be part of what was happening up there." Then, suddenly, Phelps accepted Notre Dame's offer and Crotty was no longer so sure of his future. "It was incredible," he says. "Digger actually left the day after my birthday. He had tried to call me that night, to let me know before it was made public, but I wasn't home. I didn't find out until the next day while I was riding in a car with a recruiter from Manhattan. The news came over the radio and the guy said, 'Come on, I'll take you to Jackie Powers and you can sign with us right now.' I told him I had better wait, that I needed to think things over, but it really didn't take me long. I decided I was sold more on Digger than Fordham. He told me I should go to Fordham, but I told him I wanted to play for him."

After his freshman and sophomore seasons, however, it is obvious that Crotty will never be the super player many expected him to be. He neither shoots as well as Paterno nor rebounds as well as Dantley.

Goose Novak is better established, if only because he is a two-year starter. Two years after Phelps' boss at Penn tried to recruit the intelligent LaSalle, Illinois, standout for the Quakers, Digger was coaching him in his first year at Notre Dame. Novak was the team's leading scorer and rebounder that sophomore season. Last year, when his former freshman teammate Shumate joined the varsity, he moved from center to forward, sacrificing his offensive game to concentrate on defense. "That first year was like a nightmare," he says, "and it got harder and harder to keep up our morale. But Digger convinced us that if we did our best, we would be better the next year." Novak says he had three ambitions when he came to Notre Dame: to excel academically and qualify for medical school, to contribute to the school's basketball program, and to play on a national championship team. Gary is a good student without being an intellectual, a good player without all the natural skills. He succeeds in both through earnest dedication.

There is no freshman capable of challenging John Shumate for his position. Aggressive and domineering in personality and style of play, Shu was the team's leading scorer and rebounder last year and the Most Valuable Player in the NIT. Shumate was born in South Carolina, the son of an evangelical preacher, but he grew up street-wise in Elizabeth, New Jersey. He did not begin playing basketball until his sophomore year at Thomas Jefferson High School, but his record-setting performances soon won him wide acclaim.

If Shumate had followed the advice of his high school principal, he would have gone to Fordham and played under Phelps. As it happened, he took his parents' advice to leave the metropolitan area and quite accidentally caught up with Phelps at Notre Dame after his freshman season was over.

When Phelps arrived on the Notre Dame campus in the spring of 1971, he found a gifted but hostile athlete—confused, frustrated, and made ambivalent by his unfamiliar social environment. "I didn't want to come out here in the first place," Shumate says. "I preferred a black school because I had always lived around blacks. I even told my parents I'd blame them if I flunked out." The problems Shumate encountered were neither mental nor physical. His powerful play led the freshman team in scoring and rebounding, and he maintained satisfactory grades in the classroom, drawing special notice for the "depth" of his English compositions.

His real difficulty was adjusting to the social scheme of a small-town, predominantly white-male environment. "I just couldn't get used to the place. There weren't many other blacks and almost no black girls. At parties there would be about five guys to every girl. I wasn't able to get home when I wanted to and finally my mother told me to come on back. But my dad said stick it out, that it would get better."

For a long while it did not. Although there were three blacks starting on the varsity—Austin Carr, Collis Jones, and Sid Catlett—he was the only one on the freshman team. "Whites called me a token and blacks called me an Uncle

Tom," he vividly recalls. "I remember playing against Michigan State and crying right there on the court when some of their black students called me 'Uncle Tom' during the game. After it was over they came up to me and said they didn't see how I could be the only nigger on an all-white team."

Shumate wanted only to retaliate. "It was the way I had grown up. If someone struck you, you struck back. You could never give ground because that would be a sign of weakness. I became very arrogant and temperamental. I didn't want to be bothered by people. I didn't want people touching me. I was bitter, man, very bitter. I was going a bad route."

When he became aware of Shumate's problems that first spring, Phelps made the quick and obvious judgment that if the 6′ 9″, 235-pound center were to help Notre Dame basketball, he would have to help Shumate. The new coach called him into his office, and they talked for more than three hours. Phelps told the freshman he held him in the highest regard as an athlete and a young man, that he expected no problems when both of them returned for their first season together the following year. "But," he said, "you've got to win the students and the team over to your side and you've got to win yourself over too." Shumate says it was all very strange to him. "I had always felt my high school coach would be the only one I could ever be close to. And here was Digger really trying to help me."

After another summer of perfecting his game on the asphalt playgrounds in the metropolitan area, Shumate returned to South Bend in the fall of 1971 eager for a fresh start. Maybe Notre Dame was not so bad after all. Maybe it was just getting used to it, as Austin Carr, the school's all-time leading scorer, did when he wanted to leave during *his* freshman year. "I began to see for the first time what I fully understand now, that the disadvantages I saw were really irrelevant," he says. "The important thing was to get the good education I knew Notre Dame could give me. It meant something that athletes here were getting their degrees and going on to good jobs. I'm not sure that just anybody should come here, but if a person does and it suits him he'll be all right. Notre Dame prepares you for life and that's what's so scary about it. If you give up here you could give up out there."

Phelps' reclamation project was not complete, but it was progressing. Then, just after the start of preseason practice, an unexpected and tragic discovery changed everything. Shumate seemed easily fatigued in the early workouts. He was short of breath and there was a tightness in his left leg. Tests determined a clot in the sore limb, and a virus infection in the sac around his heart. The clot could not be treated until the infection subsided. Shumate lay in the intensive-care room of the hospital for nine days, his condition growing more serious. He lost forty pounds. Basketball no longer seemed very important. "Digger came to see me and said I should only worry about getting well," remembers Shumate. "More than ever I knew he was trying to help me. It may sound corny, but I decided this is one man I was going to win for."

When Shumate finally recovered it was several more months before he could regain his strength and stamina, causing him to miss his sophomore season. Now, two years later, he says he is not as quick as he once was, that he has lost some of his coordination. He says that, though nobody really believes him. His blend of strength and finesse underneath is rare and his outside shooting excellent.

Gary Brokaw came out of New Jersey high school basketball with a reputation exceeding Shumate's. He was an All-American at New Brunswick High and once scored sixty points in a game. After a freshman season in which the 6' 3" guard averaged twenty-eight points per game, there were inevitable comparisons with Austin Carr. "That might have put pressure on me if it hadn't been for Digger," Brokaw says. "He told me to play my own game and not to worry about what other people were saying." Brokaw's fluid ease and slick, smooth moves won him the nickname Magic, and he likes it. What he does not like is the way he played last year when his average fell to seventeen points per game. "I know I can do better. My shooting percentage was much lower than it should be." Brokaw believes the team will also improve. "It took us a while to get things together last year because so many of us were sophomores. Now we're older and with new players like Dantley we're going to be even better. My goal is to make the final four of the NCAA tournament."

Brokaw and Dwight Clay had their initial contacts with Notre Dame when Johnny Dee was still coach, but it was Phelps who signed them. Brokaw, in fact, did not visit Notre Dame until the week Dee resigned. Clay's interest in the Irish had little to do with either coach, since he initiated contact with the school himself through his assistant coach at Fifth Avenue High in Pittsburgh. "I just wanted to go to Notre Dame," he says.

The 6' Clay is the quarterback of the Irish team, a responsibility unrelated to his personal scoring or rebounding statistics. His job is to run the offense, hit the open man, be aware of whatever offensive or defensive strategy Phelps may want during the flow of play. The assignment suits his unruffled personality and his personality suits his nickname, the Iceman. It was the Iceman who ended Marquette's eighty-one-game home winning streak with a late basket on January 13, and it was the Iceman four days later against Pittsburgh, with a twenty-five-footer at the regulation buzzer that led the Irish to an eventual 85–76 overtime victory. The cool in Dwight's personality is studied—protective coloration. The reticent Brokaw comes by his more naturally.

\* \* \*

Every team needs one player to run the show and, for us, Dwight is the man. Because of this I try to maintain a special relationship with him. He must know what I want, and I must understand his capabilities and show my confidence in him. Dwight is most effective when we're pressing and running. He really turns on in those situations and excites the fans.

## FRIDAY, OCTOBER 19

The threat of freshman competition felt by several of Notre Dame's veteran players is justified. Adrian Dantley is a 6′ 5″, 225-pound bull with uncommon grace. Bill Paterno's shooting ability from long range is as perfect as his form. Toby Knight seems to always come up with the ball around the basket. Ray Martin does not shoot as well as either Bill Drew or Dave Kuzmicz, but he has great potential as a floor general and in the pressing game. Today's practice is a showcase for these skills. In a series of round-robin scrimmages among the returning starters, the freshmen, and the third-string team, the young players finish a strong second. The performance is not lost on the coaches as they shower in their private dressing room afterwards. "Impressive," says Phelps.

Off the court, however, things are not going quite so well for the freshmen, who are feeling the strain of independence. Dantley's calls to his mother in Washington are frequent. Martin is in regular contact with his high school coach at Mater Christi in Long Island City, New York. Bill Drew wonders if he can be one of the boys without joining them for a beer at Corby's. Each copes in his own way with unfamiliar athletic, academic, and social pressures. It's such a change from a few short months ago when they were celebrated by their communities and courted by recruiters from all over the country.

None had received as much attention as Dantley, whose reputation attracted three hundred callers. He was the first freshman ever to start at DeMatha High School, a prep power of long standing in the Washington area under Morgan Wootten. Dantley wiped out school scoring, rebounding, and free-throw shooting records, and became only the second player ever named to the All-Metropolitan team three times. He was an All-American twice and was the Most Valuable Player in six tournaments, including the nation's premier schoolboy all-star event, the Dapper Dan Classic in Pittsburgh.

Dantley chose Notre Dame from a final group that also included North Carolina State, Maryland, and Minnesota. The latter was actually his mother's favorite. His decision was so long in coming the NCAA investigated to see if he was playing one illegal offer against another. "There were some things said by different schools in a very sly way," Dantley says, "but I wasn't looking for anything." So Adrian eventually chose Notre Dame by first eliminating the competition. "North Carolina State was my second choice but the only good thing about it was the basketball team," he says. "I decided against Maryland because Lefty Driesell made everything such a hassle. He was the worst of all the coaches. He would call just about every night and wouldn't let me off the phone. All he did was make me mad." In contrast to Driesell, Dantley found Phelps almost distant. "Digger only called me three or four times all year, and when I visited here in early May he kept his cool and didn't bug me," Dantley says. "And I thought he was more honest and sincere than a lot of coaches. I just liked the way he said things."

A more important factor was quite coincidental. Dantley was heavily influenced by several Washington area basketball players who encouraged him to follow in their footsteps to Notre Dame. One was Sid Catlett; three more were Austin Carr, Bob Whitmore, and Collis Jones—the first, third, and fifth leading scorers in Notre Dame history. Carr and Jones, in fact, drove all night from the East Coast just to be in South Bend when Dantley visited. "I had played basketball with those guys on the playground and I trusted them," Dantley says. "They warned me how tough it would be and said I'd just have to stick it out. But they encouraged me to come and I did."

Dantley has found the problems to be as real as everyone promised. "The adjustment has been tremendous and right now with midterm exams coming up, I'm really worried about my grades. Sometimes I wonder if I shouldn't have gone to an easier school where I could have gotten some money. But I'm going to stick it out."

Boyish Bill Paterno shares Dantley's concern about his academic standing but, also like Dantley, he has come to Notre Dame confident of winning a starting forward position. "I think I can beat one of them out," he says. "That's why I came here." Paterno could have gone elsewhere, of course; such is the demand for 6' 5" All-America forwards who lead their high school teams (in his case, Christian Brothers Academy in Lincroft, New Jersey) to three straight state championships. One school was particularly sweet on "Apple" Paterno. Its representative talked of credit cards, country club memberships, and frequent air transportation home. "It all sounded pretty good until I talked to Digger," he says. "He told me there would be nothing like that at Notre Dame, but that earning a degree here would mean a lot in the future."

Academics are less a problem for Ray Martin, a high school honor student and basketball All-American. Though he set the career scoring record at Mater Christi, his real skills are playmaking and defense. On a team where Afros and near-Afros dominate, his hair is unfashionably short. Bill Drew built a strong academic record at Centereach (New York) High School, and he has an outside shot that rivals Paterno's. Dave Kuzmicz, the local boy from St. Joseph's High School in South Bend, is adjusting to his new guard position. Toby Knight, a 6′ 9″ All-American at Port Jefferson (New York) High School on Long Island, is at a disadvantage when competing against the other, more experienced and aggressive frontcourt players. Still, his averages of thirty points and twenty rebounds a game last year indicate future potential.

*  *  *

I'm against the freshman rule. If I had a real choice our freshmen wouldn't be eligible for the varsity, much less competing for starting positions. But the NCAA says that freshmen can play so I have to let them, even though I strongly believe they can be hurt by it unless precautions are taken.

I'm not surprised that several of the new players are worried about making it here. The academic pressures are very real—and it was no different in the Ivy League. No matter how impressive our players' backgrounds had been at Penn, it was a great strain on them too. And they weren't even competing against the varsity. So add athletic competition to unfamiliar academic and social environments and you have the potential for real problems.

We follow the freshman rule reluctantly and try to stay aware of our players' progress. Frankly, we only let our freshmen play varsity ball because the schools we compete against do. I wouldn't have much success recruiting players if I told them they could only play three years at Notre Dame, when everywhere else but the Ivy League they could play four. Most of them would laugh me right out of their homes.

I would like to see the freshman rule reexamined after it has been in effect for four years—determine how many kids stayed in school and graduated and how many gave up and transferred somewhere else or quit to play pro basketball. The freshman rule was instituted last year, and the first class to graduate under it will finish in the spring of 1976. If the rate of attrition is higher for four years of eligibility than it was for three, then I think some changes are in order.

## SATURDAY, OCTOBER 20–SUNDAY, OCTOBER 21

Digger and Terry have flown East for a football game against Army—which Notre Dame wins 62–3—and homecoming celebrations in Beacon, New York, and at Rider College in Trenton.

Digger, the oldest of three children, was born and raised in Beacon, where his mother and father remain. He was an outstanding athlete in the class of '59 at Beacon High School and, later, a member of the volunteer hook-and-ladder firefighting company. Two special reminders of this community of thirteen thousand hang on his office wall in South Bend. One is a plaque, presented January 16, 1971, when the town celebrated "Digger's Day," and the other is a silver shovel, given three months later, "for achievements in the field of coaching which have brought pride and recognition to the Beacon-Fishkill area." At Jimmy Gallagher's Shell station and Mi-Ro's Bar, they love the Digger.

Nor have they forgotten him at Rider College, where, with limited scholarship help, he received undergraduate and graduate degrees in business in 1963 and 1964. Phelps, a bench-warmer his senior year when Rider won the NAIA District 31 championship, is honored at a Saturday night banquet as this year's outstanding alumnus. The plaque cites "distinguished and exceptional attainment in life, thereby reflecting glory and credit on the college."

* * *

This was some weekend. I must say, however, that although I am flattered by the award I have no idea what I did to deserve it. Maybe it was Rider's way of thanking me for my year as a graduate assistant coach because at the time I got absolutely nothing for it. Looking back, though, it was certainly worth it. I got a good education and a taste of college coaching experience. And I married the homecoming queen.

It was especially nice to get back to Beacon. Everyone's home town should be as relaxing, peaceful, and friendly. Years ago my mother's family owned quite a bit of land in this area, but in time they lost it. The year I coached at Fordham, Terry and I lived in Beacon and I drove back and forth every day. It was exactly fifty-three miles one way, along the Hudson River, past old castles overlooking the road, right by the Babe Ruth field I played on as a kid. Terry and I even bought a house that year—at the foot of Mount Beacon—but we lived in it only eight months before I got the Notre Dame job.

The best thing about coming home, of course, is seeing friends and family. Tom Layden, my first coach at Rider, is teaching in the business department now. Mother is in her usual good spirits and things are going well for Dad, the original and still practicing "Digger" after thirty-five years in the undertaking business. I also was able to see Jimmy Gallagher and my high school buddy, Norm Schofield. I still call him Caesar because he was even worse in Latin than I was. People here always ask about Dick DiBiaso, since he coached successfully at Beacon High School his first six years after graduation from Mansfield State. That's how I met him, and I can still remember the two of us talking about coaching a college team to the national championship some day. Such dreams. Dick even married my girl-next-door, Shawna Farley. She actually lived across the street, but it is a funny coincidence. Anyway, it's good to be home.

## MONDAY, OCTOBER 22

The second week of basketball practice marks the start of public relations appearances by Phelps that will last until the season begins and pick up again in the spring. Immediate priority goes to the campus residence halls—Morrisey, Stanford, Grace, Keenan, Fisher, wherever he receives an invitation. Then there are the civic groups—the South Bend Lions, the South Bend Rotary, the Ladies of Notre Dame. They are more selectively accepted. The usual format includes a discussion of the team's prospects, a question-and-answer session, and perhaps a game film from last season.

Phelps' easy wit belies his serious approach to life and makes him a popular choice for speaking engagements. His customary fee for the more formal off-campus occasions is five hundred dollars, a nice supplement to his coach's salary, which is modest by big-time basketball standards. Phelps, in the third year of a four-year contract, is making twenty thousand dollars, following the second of two specified annual increases of one thousand dollars each. His income is further supplemented by a weekly television show on WNDU and two summer basketball camps he and his assistants conduct, one on campus and one back East. He keeps his sporty wardrobe up to date by doing commercials for Gilbert's, a local men's store, and he drives a new Thunderbird provided by Joe Hayden Ford, the cosponsor of his television show. In short, he is comfortable but by no means wealthy.

\* \* \*

Coaching is a high-risk occupation, especially since we don't have tenure. If a good coach put the effort into making money that he does into building a winning program, he could be a wealthy businessman. As it is, we deserve whatever we can make as long as we fulfill the responsibilities and obligations that go with the job.

Very important among them, I believe, are my public relations contacts with students, alumni, and other groups interested in Notre Dame. I especially want the students to get behind what we are trying to do. There is nothing better than the support an enthusiastic student body can bring. We had it at Penn and Fordham and we have it here. Everything you've heard about Notre Dame spirit is true, and it doesn't just apply to football. It exists because the students know that our basketball players are athletes only a few hours each day; the rest of the time they are no different from anyone else. People get behind you when they respect and appreciate what you are trying to do. Without them there is no such thing as a home-court advantage.

Alumni support is an outgrowth of student support. Every spring, I attend alumni meetings in different parts of the country to encourage donations to the school's general fund. The athletic department's operational expenses are drawn from this fund, but everything we make is put back in. Fortunately, the intercollegiate program here shows a profit.

Alumni also help us in recruiting, though I don't mean illegally. I might ask an alumnus to introduce himself to the family of a prospect, just so they can see what the finished product of a Notre Dame education looks like —let them ask him questions and find out what he thinks about the place. Every school does this, but you have to be very careful that some zealot doesn't get you into trouble.

Alumni often provide summer jobs for our players. Dwight Clay worked in a brewery this past summer, and Gary Brokaw worked for a businessman in his home town. Ray Martin got a job with the Woolworth chain because Aubrey Lewis, one of its vice presidents, is a Notre Dame graduate. Some other jobs were arranged, but not all of them were filled. John Shumate, for instance, had a job in the shipyards, but he didn't work because he was tied up with other commitments. We got Myron Schuckman a job in Kansas City, but he preferred to stay on his family's farm in McCracken.

We usually come through for the players, but it's tough. I remember Clay saying, "Coach, I don't know if I want to lift beer cases all summer." I told him, "Dwight, if you find something better, let me know."

## TUESDAY, OCTOBER 23

The balance between academic responsibility and athletic opportunity at Notre Dame is a delicate one. Today it tilts sharply in a direction that might surprise many critics of major college sports. Responding to a letter from Dr. Joseph

W. Scott of the school's sociology department, Phelps writes, "I personally feel that if he [Adrian Dantley] is not doing his work academically he should not practice basketball. I know basketball means a lot to him, yet he has to understand it is only a small part of his life."

The message is clear. There is no attempt to pressure Dr. Scott into compromising his role as an educator, and no admonition to "give the kid a break." Quite obviously if Adrian Dantley or anyone else cannot make it in the classroom, there is no place for him on the basketball floor. At least, not at Notre Dame.

The academic progress of Irish athletes is closely monitored by Mike DeCicco, an engineering professor and successful fencing coach. Four times each semester, all of Notre Dame's 417 athletes are evaluated by their professors. Is the student doing *A, B, C, D,* or *F* work? Is he going to class and paying attention? Does he need a tutor? Following midsemester examinations DeCicco sends out "pink slips" to report grade results. "The important thing about all this," says DeCicco, a round little man with a passion for W. C. Fields, "is that the kids realize I know what they are doing. You've got to understand that athletes are born optimists. They think they can make a comeback in the classroom the way they do in a game. Well, it just isn't true. My main job is seeing to it that they keep up and don't fall behind."

Right now DeCicco's major project is Dantley, who is being helped along in math, physics, and sociology by several of the two dozen or so graduate and undergraduate tutors working for the athletic department. The academic requirements that a Notre Dame basketball player must meet are strict. He must do more than pass; after his freshman year he must attain a solid *C* average every semester. "When I first took the job, I thought this criterion was too strict," says DeCicco. "I fought the 2.0 in favor of a 1.6 average so we could stay competitive with our opponents. I said we should play with the same deck of cards, but Fr. Joyce wouldn't go along. He said we would not compromise ourselves. Now, by doing it this way, an athlete is almost certain to graduate. He needs the same grade average to get his degree that he does to play sports. That's why we graduate nearly every athlete who stays out for a team."

There are the inevitable academic casualties, of course, but there are also the good students like Gary Novak. "Gary has a really good chance of being awarded an NCAA postgraduate scholarship," says DeCicco. "Only athletes at Yale and the Air Force Academy have won more than ours."

*  *  *

Academics is something I feel very strongly about. I was certainly not a scholar myself, but I did learn the importance of a college education. Unfortunately, many high schools graduate students who are completely unprepared for college work. Some kids just don't know how to study for an exam, or take notes, or properly express themselves in a term paper.

Mike DeCicco does an excellent job of counseling and tutoring Notre Dame's athletes. He can't hide anyone in gut courses, and we don't even offer a physical education major. An athlete here is either in Arts and Letters, Science, Engineering, or Business Administration, and he must take at least twelve hours each semester.

Our academic requirements make us more selective in our recruiting than most schools. I don't mean there are eighteen geniuses on the team, but our so-called marginals would get along very well at most other places. To be considered for Notre Dame, a high school senior needs a solid college preparatory background: at least two years of a foreign language, three years of math, four years of English, and one year of science. I went all the way to Oklahoma once to try to convince a prospect that if he were really interested in Notre Dame, he would take his third year of math. Not until these requirements are fulfilled does the admissions office look at class rank, college board scores, and IQ.

Thirteen of the country's top twenty high school prospects are below our standards. I won't present any player to our dean of admissions unless he has a good chance of being accepted. If he is marginal, he must be willing to cooperate with DeCicco and do the academic work. He can be counseled and tutored, and he may miss practice if it conflicts with his class schedule, but every athlete must understand what will be expected of him academically.

The member schools of the NCAA were wrong to repeal the rule requiring a high school senior to project at least a 1.6 college grade average. With class rank and College Boards no longer considered, an athlete can make Cs in shop courses and still qualify for a scholarship at many schools. Notre Dame, however, will always follow a higher standard, even if it beats us. And sometimes it does.

## WEDNESDAY, OCTOBER 24

A college athlete must order his priorities very soon after settling on campus and at Notre Dame the choices are limited. To play he must study, and to study he must restrict his social life. Given the conditions in South Bend, social lethargy is easily accomplished, though Brokaw is probably overstating the problem when he says, "All I do here is eat, sleep, study, and play basketball." To be sure, Brokaw has grown accustomed to this place. There are only 2,296 women on the Notre Dame and adjacent St. Mary's campuses—a 5 to 2 ratio—and 47 of them are black.

Dantley and the other freshmen are still learning. In the afternoon before today's practice Adrian leaves his room on the ground floor of Fisher dormitory—a popular residence because it is beside the cafeteria—and walks down the hall to Shumate's. For a while the two sit quietly absorbing the music in a rumpled room so narrow that, if John were standing in the middle, he could almost touch the opposite walls. Finally, Dantley asks a question.

"Hey, Shu, how come you never told me there weren't any girls around here?"

"Man, if I had, you wouldn't have come."

At Notre Dame, a girl friend is the last female you dated back home or the first (if any) you meet at a Saturday night dormitory bash.

There are other alternatives, but the school's broad schedule of lectures, seminars, colloquiums, workshops, and exhibits is not what the average athlete has in mind when he wants relief from his basketball and classroom regimen.

Not unexpectedly, the players find diversion among themselves in black and white cliques that closely reflect ethnic backgrounds and interests. The ongoing experiment in Room 220 of Flanner Tower between Long Island freshmen Bill Drew and Toby Knight is on the verge of breakup—not because one is white and the other is black, but because their tastes in music differ.

The five black players in Fisher Hall—Shumate, Brokaw, Clay, Dantley, and Martin—are a more homogeneous group. For them, a night out means crowding into Brokaw's five-year-old Volkswagen to replenish their snack supply at McDonald's or a supermarket. "Clay's a little different," says Shumate. "He goes but he doesn't buy very much. He just knocks on your door around midnight and asks if there are any potato chips left."

Another separate-but-equal group holds out in a suite in Grace Tower, a high-rise dormitory near the huge Memorial Library building on the newer part of campus. Chris "Hawk" Stevens, Ken "Geek" Wolbeck, Greg Schmelzer, and Gary "Goose" Novak form an uninhibited coterie of seniors whose nights out sometimes include Crotty, Paterno, and Kuzmicz. As a group, they pop more than enough tops to make up for the cans pushed away by abstainers like Dantley, Drew, and Shumate.

Whatever the choice, Big Macs and Tall Buds are more fun than cold showers.

\* \* \*

All right, so Notre Dame is no bachelor's paradise. We warn the players this isn't a country club when they are recruited. I am sure it is especially dull for blacks. But I believe they prefer Notre Dame's academic and athletic advantages to its social drawbacks. As for the school's acceptance of blacks, the long and active civil rights leadership of our president, Fr. Theodore Hesburgh, speaks for itself.

My influence as coach changes when the players leave the basketball court and classroom. As long as they act responsibly, I don't try to run their private lives. But I do have certain guidelines that I want them to follow. When we began practice a week and a half ago, I expected everyone to be mentally and physically ready to play. For the best players, basketball is a year-round game, not just a winter pastime.

Once the season begins, all of us, players and coaches alike, should be very conscious of our public images. This is why I wear my hair a little shorter this time of year. A neat, well-groomed team won't win any basketball games because it looks nice, but it might make an alumnus more willing to contribute money if he thinks we're teaching proper discipline. My policy on in-season drinking is also dictated by what others may think. If a player wants to have a beer, he'd better be sure of two things: I don't know about it, and it won't affect his play. If I see him, I am going to enforce discipline. And if he doesn't play well, even after only one drink, anyone else who saw him will say, "No wonder the guy shot three for twenty; he got bombed last night." Again, this same rule applies to myself. You'll never see me drinking a beer the day of a game. I want to make all of my mistakes cold sober.

My guidelines are not much different from those of any other coach. However, I do differ with coaches who tell players where they should live, what they should do with their free time, and what they should wear. I'm opposed to jock dorms. It's very healthy that Roger Anderson and Myron Schuckman are the only players in Keenan and Stanford Halls. Even if they are each 6′ 9″ tall they aren't always going to be basketball players. On the other hand, we rotate roommate assignments on the road so the players will get to know each other better.

Something else I don't like is a team decked out in eighteen identical pairs of pants, blazers, and ties. Of course it is necessary for a player to sacrifice some of his individuality in order to promote teamwork, but to dress everyone alike is taking the thing too far. As much as I enjoy colorful clothes, I am not about to tell my players they can't express their own personalities with their own outfits. I wouldn't even recognize Brokaw and Clay in blue blazers. At home they can wear whatever they like, and on the road we just ask that they wear a tie or turtleneck.

# THURSDAY, OCTOBER 25

As usual, when Phelps arrives at work shortly after nine o'clock, assistant coaches McLaughlin and DiBiaso are already at their desks. Such promptness at this time of year is not really necessary. Not until the season starts does the pace quicken and the burden of demands grow. In October and November there are no opponents to scout, no prospects to visit, no game plans to prepare. But there are always letters to be written or phone calls to be made and, by ten o'clock, when Phelps has finished going through his correspondence with Dottie, the assistants gather in Digger's office to outline the afternoon's two-and-a-half-hour practice. It is in these meetings that players are evaluated, strategies discussed, and techniques suggested. And it is also here that the working relationship of the three men becomes clear.

Though DiBiaso and McLaughlin are paid almost the same salaries and are said to have similar responsibilities, they play distinctly different roles in the Notre Dame program. Of the two, DiBiaso is much more assertive, which gives him more apparent influence. McLaughlin may have been with Digger at Fordham and Notre Dame both, but DiBiaso is older and more experienced and has known Phelps longer. It is not coincidental that the office adjoining the head coach's is DiBiaso's.

DiBiaso, in fact, would very much like to be a head coach himself. After three years at Virginia and in this, his third year at Notre Dame, he is suffering the not-uncommon anxiety of any experienced assistant with a wife and two children. For now, at least, McLaughlin is young, single, not as self-assured, and less ambitious.

* * *

There are not many things more important to the success of a program than dedicated, hard-working, knowledgeable assistant coaches. I know every head coach will tell you this, but I really believe I have the two best assistants in the country.

I have to feel this way because I depend on them so much. I couldn't stand to have a couple of yes-men around. Dick and Frank are aggressive and independent, but when a final decision is made, they go along 100 percent. I want their opinions, but I also want their loyalty.

During practice Dick works more with the forwards and centers, and Frank, the guards. Although both scout and recruit, Dick is the coordinator, just as Frank sets up the summer camps. Each recommends strategy in meetings and during games, and very often I follow their suggestions. Because they know my philosophy so well, they can anticipate my thinking and act accordingly.

You may wonder what is left for me to do. For better or worse, I make the final decisions. Dick may draw up the list of high school prospects, initiate contact with them, and determine who among them we should be interested in, but the final decision of whom we go after the hardest is mine. Frank can come back with a thick scouting report on a team recommending all kinds of offensive and defensive strategies, but unless I'm convinced they suit our personnel and the players we are going up against, we'll do it some other way.

Obviously a lot of the credit that belongs to an assistant is given to the head coach, whether it's winning a game or recruiting a player. But it's also true that nobody ever fired an assistant because a team was losing.

## FRIDAY, OCTOBER 26

Tomorrow the Notre Dame football team will play Southern California, the unbeaten, once-tied defending national champion which last fall inflicted a 45–23 embarrassment on the Irish. Tonight about five thousand frenzied students gather near Stepan Center for a pep rally. The usual exhortations for victory are made, the usual declarations of preeminence offered. And who should be standing among the cheering mass but the Notre Dame basketball coach?

\* \* \*

You'd better believe I'm a Notre Dame football fan. I want Ara's team to be as successful as I want my own to be. Win or lose, I have the greatest respect for Ara as a man and coach. He's already won a national championship and I haven't come close.

Some people think there is a lot of competition and rivalry between football and basketball here. Nothing could be more wrong, although that sort of thing does occur elsewhere. Our relationship with football is excellent and I have never felt that Ara was given advantages I didn't have. We're nobody's stepchildren.

## SATURDAY, OCTOBER 27

Notre Dame 23–Southern California 14.

\* \* \*

'Twas a great day for the Irish. 'Twas also a great day to have three top high school recruits sitting on the 50-yard line.

The visitors are Dave Batton, a 6′ 10″ center from Springfield High, near Philadelphia; Donald "Duck" Williams, a 6′ 2″ guard from Mackin High in Washington, D.C.; and Mark Olberding, a 6′ 7″ forward from Melrose High in Melrose, Minnesota. Their visits could not have come at a better time. I can't tell them anything about the spirit and excitement of playing for Notre Dame that they won't see for themselves this weekend.

All recruiting visits are generally the same. Each prospect is hosted by a varsity player who shows him around, answers questions, and takes him to parties. Batton's host is Paterno, Williams' is Dantley, and Olberding's is Anderson. Of course, the coaches also talk to the visitors, but it is too early in the year for us to make our biggest recruiting pitch. Anything we say in the fall is probably forgotten by the time their decisions are made in the spring. For now, we prefer that they look around and get a feel for the school and the people.

We do require, however, that each prospect meet with Admissions Director Myron Busby and Academic Counselor Mike DeCicco. As I said before, we are very careful about whom we present for admission. Only three big men among the top fifteen in the country meet our minimum standards. The other twelve include a very highly recruited senior who has low grades in a non-college-preparatory curriculum, no College Board scores, and a ranking in the bottom 15 percent of his class. Needless to say, we haven't contacted him.

The third week of practice concludes the first half of pre-season drills. Now is the time to examine, evaluate, and adjust. Tactics and personnel must be complementary parts in a finely tuned machine. John Wooden has won nine of the last ten NCAA championships with big men and little men, high posts and low posts—the perfect fit for every occasion.

The responsibility reminds Phelps of a fantasy certain to go unfulfilled. While sitting in his office, listening to soft music from his AM-FM stereo, he says, "I would like to be the conductor of a great symphony orchestra. Isn't it like coaching? One man is trying to create beautiful music by directing instruments with vastly different sounds. He can't succeed unless every person plays his part perfectly, and he must decide which part is best for each one. I don't know anything about music, but I do know the disappointment of a bad performance."

The Athletic and Convocation Center practice floor is no concert stage, but the Irish basketball team is in daily rehearsal for a December 1 opening.

\* \* \*

We are trying to develop a style of play based on my philosophy as a coach and the particular skills of my players. Fortunately, we have some very talented individuals who seem suited to what I want to do.

I have never had such all-round depth and ability. With the addition of the freshmen, we can go eight or nine deep and, unlike last year, there won't be five men playing forty minutes a game. One of my biggest jobs will be convincing the starters it is in the best interests of the team for them to sacrifice individual points and playing time. I've never had dissension and I don't want it now.

Our new depth will let us press more often and for longer periods of time. I can remember last year Goose looking at me with his tongue hanging out and saying, "When are we going to take it off, Coach?" This season that shouldn't be a problem, because we'll just bring in fresh players like Ray Martin and Toby Knight. Dantley and Paterno, on the other hand, don't have as much speed and quickness, but they would be very effective in a power game when we need a lot of muscle.

Although different lineup combinations are possible, every player is expected to know all of the defenses. We depend on variations of four: an aggressive man-to-man with constant pressure on the ball, a fullcourt press, a halfcourt press, and a halfcourt zone. I include the halfcourt zone, even though I don't like to use it because it slows down our tempo.

Believe it or not, one of our biggest problems with the press last year was our free-throw shooting. We only made 63 percent from the line, and that isn't close to the 70 percent that we'd like. Our strategy has always been to press after a field goal or free throw, but if you miss the foul shot you don't have a chance to set it up. Of course, even if you do get into the press, it can be beaten by quick guards using short passes to bring the ball up court. This is why we were so effective last year against pressure defenses. Clay and Brokaw both have the necessary quickness and ball-handling ability, and it looks like Martin will be that kind of player, too.

I view offense a little differently than defense, probably because I was never a very good offensive player myself. Defensively, I think a team must have sound commitments and rules. Offensively, I'm more freelance-oriented. I like a fast-paced offensive game that takes advantage of the players' individual skills. Brokaw's, for example. There is no way a coach can teach those moves.

It takes years of work on the playground to develop them. And when a behind-the-back pass or a double-clutch move to the basket becomes part of a player's game, you take advantage of it; you don't tell him to cool it because that wasn't done twenty years ago or because you can't do it yourself.

My job is to develop an entire offense around the individual talents of every player. I know already I'm better off than I have been in the past because Shumate is the first outstanding big man I've ever coached. Even though he is smaller at 6′ 9″ than most of the players he goes up against, I know that if Dwight can get the ball to him, he'll use his great touch and strength to put it in the basket.

I don't mean that I want five players going one-on-one. Of course, there are rules to follow. But our patterns let the kids play their game; they don't force someone to pass up a ten-foot shot on the chance he might get another one six inches closer. The important thing is that players and coaches both read the other team's defense and make adjustments during the game.

Another problem we had last year involved players standing around on offense. When this happens, movement is lost and the defense can sag on Shumate. We've talked about this in our staff meetings and we feel we can correct it by putting in more screens and action away from the ball. This will also eliminate any tendency to overemphasize one-on-one moves. A player shouldn't think he is in the game only when he has the ball in his hands. If he wants to stand around and watch, let him buy a ticket and sit in the stands. Without question, we lost at times last year because we became less aggressive towards the end of the game.

You're always trying to learn from your mistakes, of course. Clay has shown much improvement as a ball-handler because he knows he had problems in this area last year. Brokaw is a very good all-around player, but he needs to be more consistent, especially in his shooting. Novak has become outstanding on defense because he realizes he doesn't have outstanding offensive ability. Crotty really began to come on at the end of last season with his scoring and rebounding, but he still hasn't completely made the adjustment from high school center to college forward. Shumate doesn't have any limitations offensively, but he has weaknesses defensively.

Although the freshmen are still showing what they can do, we will probably count on them quite a bit. It's already obvious they will play more than the relatively inexperienced seniors like Ken Wolbeck, Hawk Stevens, and Greg Schmelzer. Several of the freshmen have quite a bit of potential and I want to give them a chance to develop it. Sophomores Roger Anderson and Myron Schuckman must be given that opportunity also.

## MONDAY, NOVEMBER 5

There are rumors around campus that Adrian Dantley has done poorly on his mid-semester examinations, that his physics grade is beyond repair and he will be ineligible to play. Unfortunately, much of what is being said at campus hangouts like Corby's, the Library, and Nickie's is true. Dantley is in trouble. Fortunately, the pink slips from DeCicco's office do not represent final grades. There is still time, but for the next several weeks Dantley's best one-on-one moves must be with his tutors.

"I don't know if I can do it," he tells Bob Whitmore, a Notre Dame star of the late sixties, whom Phelps got into law school and took on as a graduate assistant.

"You've got to, A. D. Talk to Digger. He'll let you miss practice."

"I can't do that, Whit. I'm overweight and I need the work. I don't want to sit on the bench."

"Look, A. D., if you don't make the grades you won't be able to dress, much less sit on the bench."

\* \* \*

Although I regret the rumors, I've told Adrian that he must want to do it. We can't make the grades for him. If he has to miss practice, then he has to.

## WEDNESDAY, NOVEMBER 7

Phelps has just finished eating dinner with Terry and the three children when the phone rings at their two-story, four-bedroom house on Peashway. The caller is Shumate, who wants to report a conversation he had earlier in the evening with the partner of a well-known New York player's agent. Because of his illness two years ago, Shumate is a junior athletically and a senior academically, a situation that makes him eligible for the NBA draft in the spring.

"The guy wants to have dinner with me after our preseason game on the seventeenth," Shumate tells Phelps. "He said he'd like to talk about representing me if I decide to go pro next year."

"He knows he's supposed to come to me first, Shu. What else did he say?"

"Well, he told me I shouldn't say anything to you, and he would give me money or a plane ticket home anytime I asked."

"He said *what?*"

"Well, that's why I'm calling you."

"Look, Shu, I'll take care of him in the morning. See, it's just like we discussed last summer. Agents are just pimps trying to make a fast buck off you. They don't care if you get into trouble and lose your eligibility."

"I know, Digger. I won't even think about it until the season is over."

* * *

I don't know when I've been so mad. If this guy really had Shu's best interests at heart, he would leave him alone until the end of the season and then approach him through me. All he wants to do is lay down five thousand dollars so he can make fifty thousand dollars. Shu doesn't need him. He doesn't need any agent.

Look at what happened to Villanova and Western Kentucky in 1971, when Howard Porter and Jim McDaniels signed with agents before the season ended. The NCAA voided their teams' finishes in the championship tournament. I'm certain Shu doesn't want to break the rules and be responsible for anything like that.

Shu can save himself a lot of hassle and worry if he waits to make up his mind. When the time comes, he should evaluate the kind of year he has had, the team that drafts him, and the offer he gets. If he does decide to leave, he won't have any trouble finding someone to give him proper financial advice. I don't know if it means anything, but the presidents of the NBA and ABA, Walter Kennedy and Mike Storen [since resigned], both went to Notre Dame.

My biggest concern is that Shu not be misled by bad

advice which could distract his play or take away his eligibility before he knows definitely what he wants to do. Obviously I would hate to see him leave, but I'll support whatever decision he makes. If money is his main concern, I hope he is aware that Austin Carr turned down $500,000 as a junior, played as a senior, and then signed for $1,000,000.

## THURSDAY, NOVEMBER 8

Phelps is steaming when he calls the New York agent's office. The conversation is brief but direct. "Get lost!"

\*   \*   \*

I think I was able to get my points across. I guaranteed them that they would never work with Shumate, and I said I would be very surprised if they ever handled any of our players in the future. I still can't get over their blatant disregard for the NCAA rules and our established procedure.

## FRIDAY, NOVEMBER 9

The morning mail brings a touching request. Jack Bedan, a Notre Dame basketball player in the mid-1950's, has written Phelps concerning his thirteen-year-old son Greg, who was paralyzed recently in a youth league football accident. "The doctor has indicated he will not walk again but we are not accepting that," Bedan writes. "His attitude is tremendous and he has never been blue. I would appreciate a note or comment from you to Greg. We have spoken of the Irish often and had high hopes of his representing them some day. . . . I know you are very busy and I want to thank you in advance for your efforts."

This is the letter Phelps dictates to his secretary:

> Dear Greg:
>
> I have heard that you have had a serious accident. I hope that you listen to the doctors and do everything they ask you to do. Above all, be sure to keep your faith and keep asking God to help you recover. . . . I am sure that you believe that you will walk again. That will come through faith, prayer and hard work. . . . I certainly hope, Greg, that you remain strong in your mind and do the best you can in whatever God allows you to do. . . .
>
> > Sincerely,
> > Dick Phelps
> > Head Basketball Coach

*       *       *

This is always a difficult thing to do, because I never know exactly what to say. I can only hope that a little encouragement on my part will help the person feel better.

## SATURDAY, NOVEMBER 10

With the football team at Pittsburgh defeating the Panthers 31–10, all is quiet in South Bend. Digger and Terry had planned an evening out in Chicago, but after a two-hour drive they find that the play they had hoped to see has been canceled. Instead, they enjoy a long, private dinner, a rare moment in the hectic lives both of them lead.

Only in recent years has Digger fully appreciated Terry's strong desire to step out of his shadow and establish her own identity. He has always known what he wanted; now he knows better what she wants. At twenty-nine, Terry is sorting herself out from the myriad roles she plays: wife, mother, hostess, graduate student, and aspiring poet. Born in England, she moved to the United States in 1947, grew up in New Jersey, and became a citizen last September. She met Digger at Rider College, where she was studying biology, and they were married in 1964. As Digger moved from Pennsylvania to Fordham to Notre Dame, she pulled their growing family along, and resumed her interrupted studies in a new, albeit appropriate, area, English literature. She finally earned an undergraduate degree at Notre Dame last year, with marks high enough to merit a doctoral scholarship.

Asked once by a classmate how she took to the demands and excitement of being a coach's wife, she answered, "I would trade it tomorrow for a normal life." In fact, nothing about her life is normal. She may not have time for everything she wants, but Digger understands her need to break out, and the children are accustomed to nothing else.

"I want very much to determine my own identity," Terry asserts. "I want to be more than just a 'coach's wife' who always looks nice and says just the right thing. None of that is wrong, but I have to define myself in other ways too. Dick understands this. He knows what I am trying to do and he appreciates my independence.

"Neither of us believes our interests conflict. As much as I want to be my own person, I still try hard not to interfere with Dick's career. I know how busy he is and how much responsibility he has. I try to be careful about what I say to him. By now, I know just what he needs to hear. Sometimes it's best not to say anything. He depends on me for this."

* * *

When I became a coach, and especially after I was made a head coach, I knew I could never have a "normal home life." The distractions of the profession are too many: the travel, the social and business obligations, the worry. Many careers end, not because a coach is losing, but because he misses being around his family. I can only be thankful that my wife and family accept the difficulties involved for all of us, though I must admit my children have never known anything else. We have avoided major problems, but I would never want to make life any more difficult by becoming a professional coach.

A situation like ours gives special significance to every family occasion. When we were all in Maine last Labor Day weekend, it meant a great deal just to be together. That's the way I felt tonight when Terry and I were having dinner in Chicago. It did not matter so much what we were doing, just as long as we were doing it together, away from other people.

As you can tell, Terry is involved in a lot of things herself. She is working very hard to become more than a wife and mother and I really respect and admire her for it. It's a challenge but she is very happy doing it. When she becomes a teacher I'll be very proud. After all, Terry is an intelligent young woman who should put her mind to work. She is not really a women's libber, but she is no Middle American housewife either. Her involvement and social awareness really make her stand out.

Terry and I worry a great deal about how our outside activities affect the children. Fortunately, I have a real advantage in coaching at Notre Dame. Instead of driving 106 miles every day, as I did at Fordham, I'm home in five minutes. The other afternoon, for instance, Rick called me at the office and asked if he could come to practice. He's never done that before, but I was glad I could bring him over.

My concern for Rick, Karen, and Jennifer probably makes me more impatient and demanding with them than I should be. In traveling around, I see things I do not want happening to my own family. I'm especially concerned about drug abuse, which I think is one of the major problems in the country today. I only hope that through love, affection, and discipline my children will always want to share their problems with me.

I've learned that it's very important to make myself available to them whenever I'm home, no matter how tired I am. If Jennifer wants to talk, I'll listen. If Karen wants to show me a ballet step, I'll watch. If Rick wants to play, I'll play. That's the least I can do.


## MONDAY, NOVEMBER 12–FRIDAY, NOVEMBER 16


This is an important week for Notre Dame's freshmen. The competition is beginning to build for Saturday's exhibition game against the returning varsity, their first public test as college basketball players. Athletes live for these opportunities to show off their talents. Practice is necessary, pickup games are fun, but the essence of their sport is the crowd, the cheers, and the excitement.

The pending confrontation intensifies the purpose of the

week's practice. Phelps and his staff expect the freshmen to be more familiar with the team's different offensive and defensive tactics. After all, what a freshman team may learn in a season, varsity freshmen must master in seven weeks.

* * *

Although several of our freshmen are making a great deal of progress, I don't anticipate any lineup adjustments for Valparaiso. Saturday's intrasquad game could help me change my mind, however, especially regarding Adrian. Despite his trouble in the classroom, he is farther along than any of the other freshmen. Paterno is looking good too; he's even better as a shooter. Martin needs more work, and Drew and Kuzmicz are still catching on. Knight has spurts when he is very good and others when he is completely out of it. Toby seems to be at his best when the offense and defense are kept simple, but this is not an unusual problem for a freshman.

Sometimes a good player is unable to prove himself in his first year. We had someone like that at Pennsylvania, Bobby Morse. Even if he had been eligible, there is no way Bobby could have played as a freshman, but he developed into one of the best shooters in the country.

Pressure can really hurt a young player. This is why we've been bringing our freshmen along gradually. I'm very concerned about how they will do in our early road games at Ohio State, Northwestern, Indiana, and Kentucky. I even wonder about the adjustment capability of a player as talented as Dantley. When Adrian first got here, he was pretty cocky. I think his mother always spoiled him and he has usually had things his own way. Now he really has to work—in the classroom, which he never cared much about before, and in basketball, where he is used to being the best.

Things have not been easy the last couple of weeks, but Adrian is changing—I think for the better. He's no longer trying to get by on his reputation, and everyone respects him for it. Adrian did not dominate from the start, as people often expect a highly recruited prospect to do, but he has responded to the tough competition and proved himself to the team. Everyone, Adrian included, must understand that he is going to have both good and bad games.

## SATURDAY, NOVEMBER 17

Notre's Dame's third annual charity basketball game is a rousing success. An unexpectedly large and enthusiastic turnout of four thousand delays the start twenty minutes, but raises more than $2,300 for Thanksgiving dinners for needy South Bend families. And at $.25 or $.50 a ticket, the game is a bargain.

The veteran Gold team leads by eight points at the half but has to hold on to beat the freshmen Blues 87–84. Shumate scores twenty-four points and Novak adds twenty-two with ten rebounds. Dantley is just as impressive in a losing effort, with twenty-four points and fifteen rebounds. Although the freshmen out-rebound the veterans 53–46, they suffer grievously from poor shooting, making only 38 percent of their shots to the Golds' 55.

The impressive afternoon's showing indicates there is every bit as much depth and talent among the new players as Phelps wanted when he recruited them last spring.

*   *   *

I don't want to put too much importance on an intrasquad game, but I will say I am very encouraged. It was much closer than I expected, but I'm glad the players could put on a good show for the fans. The important thing is that we were able to raise some money for a worthy cause. The students at Notre Dame and St. Mary's who did the work deserve a lot of credit, and that includes the players too. As for myself, I just sat back and enjoyed it.

## MONDAY, NOVEMBER 19–
## SATURDAY, NOVEMBER 24

For most of Notre Dame's students, Thanksgiving week is a holiday. For the basketball players it is business as usual, though their spirits are buoyed by the release of the Associated Press preseason basketball poll, which ranks them eighth in the country. Staying up there will be a challenge, however. Sharing the Top 10 spotlight with the Irish are four of their opponents, UCLA (first, of course), Indiana (third), Marquette (seventh), and Kentucky (tenth).

The mood is exuberant on Thanksgiving afternoon when everyone gathers at Digger's house for turkey dinner and some informal camaraderie. Phelps believes occasions like this encourage team unity and give players and coaches a better understanding and appreciation of each other.

Dantley's performance in the charity game has done much to help his confidence, but it has only made Crotty appear more vulnerable. While Adrian was playing so well, Peter was managing three points and six rebounds before fouling out. As Dantley replaces Crotty in the first-team practice lineup with greater frequency, the unspoken message is becoming clearer. Peter is losing ground fast.

During one afternoon practice, a game-condition scrimmage is held with McLaughlin and DiBiaso officiating—and purposely doing a very poor job at it. In order to test the players' reaction to bad calls, a charge becomes a block, a three-second violation goes unnoticed, a pivot foot firmly planted is detected walking.

No one objects more than Shumate. After one particularly aggressive tussle underneath the basket in which he is bounced around unmercifully without a foul being called, John becomes especially annoyed.

"Come on, these guys are hanging all over me," he says disgustedly.

Finally, with about five minutes left in the scrimmage, Phelps says, "Okay, John, if you can do any better, you officiate."

Shumate takes a whistle, and before long he calls a foul on Martin. The little guard looks at him and says, "What are you talking about, Shu? I didn't commit a foul. You don't know what you're doing." The mild outburst is very much unlike Ray, except that it too is set up. Without anyone else's knowledge, Phelps had told Martin to give Shumate some grief at the first opportunity. Not until the end of practice does Phelps finally explain to John what was going on.

\* \* \*

I hope John, and the rest of the team, appreciated the little lesson we were trying to teach. A player should never let the officiating take his mind off his play. If there is any complaining to be done, I'll be the one to do it.

Actually, I have a lot of sympathy for officials. Players

are so quick and tensions are so great in games today that their job is almost impossible. I don't think it helps to use three officials either. That was tried at Big Five games in Philadelphia, and it caused more problems than it solved. The officials became too indecisive because they did not want to make each other look bad.

I honestly believe I have never won or lost a game because of officiating. Calls can certainly influence the outcome of a game, but the final score is ultimately determined by how well a team plays. UCLA would have beaten us last year, even if Bill Walton hadn't gotten away with goal-tending so often.

Don't think by this I won't criticize an official. If I see him make a bad call, he is going to hear about it—but from me, not my players or assistants. By pointing these things out, I hope the official will see it our way the next time or give us a break on some other kind of play. All I really want from an official is consistency. Walking must be the same on both sides of the floor. It should be no more physical under one basket than it is under the other. And both officials should make calls on both teams. It's amazing how often they see violations on only one end of the court.

Ideally, an official will never be too quick to blow his whistle. A good one gives a warning before he makes a call. After all, spectators don't pay to watch free-throw shooting contests. Obvious fouls should not be overlooked, but neither should incidental contact interrupt the flow of play.

It also bothers me when an official makes an incorrect call because he was either out of position or did not see the play completely develop. This is especially aggravating when it affects techniques that we are teaching in practice. A good example is the charge, which—admittedly—is sometimes very difficult to distinguish from the block. We tell our players to step in front of the dribbler and take the charge whenever they are legally able to. This is good defense, no matter what a run-and-gun offensive coach says. An official must be ready to make the correct call, not guess if the collision was caused by a block or a charge.

Since we emphasize defense, I'll point out another area where strict enforcement is particularly important to a pressing team. The offensive has only five seconds to bring the ball in bounds and ten seconds to move it into the front court. When those five or ten seconds are up, we want to hear that whistle immediately, and not one second later.

In general, I get along with officials pretty well. The ones at our home games are assigned by the Big Ten and, as a group, I think they are outstanding. On the other hand, there are some officials I would prefer not to have. It isn't unusual for personality clashes to develop when an official's style adversely affects a team's. This happened with one particular guy while I was coaching the freshman team at Penn. We were going at each other all the time, and it was not fair to the players. Finally I had to ask the league not to assign him to any more of our games and we were all better off for it.

## SUNDAY, NOVEMBER 25

Preparations for the first week of play have begun in earnest and, indications are, none too soon. In practice today, the eighth-ranked team in the country scrimmages the blue team, a prep squad of third-teamers running the Ohio State offense and defense. After twenty minutes of simulated game conditions, the nations' eighth-ranked team escapes with a 52–48 win. If the Buckeyes know their own style of play any better than Notre Dame's blues, the Irish will be in trouble on December 3.

* * *

I was more pleased with the performance of our blue team than I was disappointed that the regulars did not win by a bigger score. This is the kind of commitment we need from them. As individuals they will see very little action this year and three of them—Ken Wolbeck, Tom Varga, and Tom Hansen—won't even get to dress for home games. The other three—Chris Stevens, Greg Schmelzer, and Myron Schuckman—will be among the fifteen players dressing at home, but they won't be on the twelve-man traveling squad. This is always subject to change, but that's the way it will be for now.

Everyone has a different responsibility on this team and the blues' acceptance of such an unrewarding role is fantastic. We need these guys. They are the key to our preparation for every game. When they play well, the regulars must stay alert and aggressive. I'll make a promise right now. If we reach the final four in Greensboro I will personally see to it that the blues are down there with us—even if I have to give them my car to drive.

I know how difficult it is to sit on the bench. Even though I started at Rider as a junior, I was a substitute most of my senior season. I accepted it because I believed in the coach and trusted his judgment. He turned out to be right because we were winners that year. Chris Stevens, who started as a sophomore, is not suffering anything I have not felt myself. My job is to explain to him and the others why it has to be this way. They are no less a part of the team than anyone else.

Today's was not the first indication they are willing to make the contribution we need. On several occasions Chris and Kenny, especially, have pointed things out to the freshmen who are playing ahead of them. I don't care how trite it sounds, but this willingness to put one's own ambition and pride aside for the good of the team is essential for success. And it is expected of every player on the squad.


## MONDAY, NOVEMBER 26


In a coach's world the obligations are to people, not players. Clinging to the bottom rung of the Irish basketball ladder is Tom Hansen, a 6′ 2″ guard with no great ability. Although Tom's chief athletic interest is baseball, he came out for varsity basketball two years ago and, conditions being what they were, made the team.

Hansen even started occasionally, but he finished the year on the bench with a 2.4 scoring average. Last winter, he appeared in nine games and scored two points. Now, in his senior year, Tom has returned for more of the same drudgery and discipline. In return, he will not travel, play, or dress out. "That's okay," Hansen says stoically. "I'm going to stick it out because I like to compete, even if it's only during practice."

Despite Tom's negligible contribution to the team, a bond exists between him and Phelps.

It is just before lunch, and Digger is on the telephone with Tom Petroff, the baseball coach at Northern Colorado and a friend from their days at Rider. Because Hansen is interested in becoming a baseball coach, Phelps wonders if Petroff could use him as a graduate assistant next year. Petroff says he has no such opportunity to offer, but he suggests there might be possibilities in the South, where college baseball is bigger. "Have Tom call me," Petroff adds, "and I'll help in any way I can."

Later in the day, Gary Novak stops by to discuss his medical school ambitions. Gary is discouraged because his med boards do not measure up to his impressive classroom accomplishments. Phelps asks if he would be interested in the University of Pittsburgh. Novak says he will consider every opportunity.

"I know a doctor associated with their medical school," Phelps tells him, "and he's a Notre Dame alumnus. Let's call him and see what he says."

The doctor recommends that Gary apply and send a copy of his transcript directly to him. "If he has a chance of being accepted I'll try to help," he promises.

\* \* \*

A coach can thank a player for four years of sacrifice and hard work by insisting that he earn a degree. He should also emphasize that basketball is not a lifelong career. One of the unforgiveable crimes in college basketball today is the lack of concern many coaches have for athletes after their eligibility has expired. And, unfortunately, there are players who cannot see beyond the basketball court either.

A lot of athletes live in a fantasy world. They sit on a pedestal and think everybody owes them a living. I suppose they think they will be playing basketball in front of cheering crowds forever. I've often wondered how many high school kids really know how tough it is to win a scholarship and start for a college team. Or how many college players realize the unlikelihood of their being drafted and signed by a professional club. Somewhere along the line, somebody has got to say, "Don't count on it. The odds are against you." *

Hansen and Novak and most of the other seniors are properly concerned with their futures. The younger players are hardest to convince. Gary Brokaw's biggest problem right now is his narrowmindedness about professional ball. He can have a pro career if he really works at it, but he must realize it won't last forever. I want him to discuss this with Dick Rosenthal, who played professionally in Fort Wayne after he left Notre Dame. He's now the president of St. Joseph Bank here in town. I don't mean that Gary should necessarily go into banking, but he should be interested and involved in something. An athlete like Gary has a lot of opportunity to meet people and make contacts that can help him later on. He should take advantage of this while he is playing, because it does not take the public long to forget your name and number.

Another player I'm concerned about is Peter Crotty. I know Peter is disappointed right now in the way things are going, but he can't give up. He has told me about his interest in hospital administration, so I will try to set up some appointments for him.

The best test of a coach is not his won-lost record, but what becomes of his players. I want mine to be able to cope with society. Dick, Frank, and I try to relate to our players as big brothers who have been around long

* After Phelps discussed this problem, a survey taken by *The New York Times* indicated that the odds are almost insurmountable. Of 200,000 high school seniors playing basketball, 5,700 remain athletes as college seniors. Of these, 211 are drafted. Only 55 eventually sign contracts, making the leap from high school to professional ball a .0000275 chance.

enough to have some advice worth listening to. I was helped along by a lot of people and I would like to do the same for my players. Tom Winterbottom, for instance, gave me my start in coaching in a Beacon summer league after I graduated from Rider. Without his guiding hand, I would have ended up in embalming school.

Maybe I'm pessimistic, but I believe today's kids are confused by what is going on around them. They shouldn't accept my values for themselves, but they should learn how to cope in their own way. I want them to compete and survive—and if one of them decides to be a bum, I expect him to be the most "together" bum around.

## TUESDAY, NOVEMBER 27

Dennis T. Penny, president of the Notre Dame Club of Terre Haute, would like to see his alma mater play locally against Indiana State. "We know your schedule is very tight and that you would prefer to play higher-rated schools," Penny writes Phelps. "But I.S.U. will certainly give you a good game, comparable to those you now have scheduled."

\* \* \*

In answering Mr. Penny, I pointed out the considerations that make a series with Indiana State impossible for now. We get similar requests from alumni groups quite often, and it would be impossible to fulfill every one. The same considerations apply to scheduling proposals made by schools all over the country. In recent months we've been forced to turn down such impressive potential opponents as Minnesota, Memphis State, and Weber State. We also reject all invitations to Christmas tournaments.

This year's schedule is a good example of the kind we like to play. First of all, fifteen of our twenty-six games are at home. This is an ideal arrangement because home games give us a partisan crowd and more money—about twenty thousand dollars a game. (We keep nearly all the gate and concession receipts and there are no travel expenses.) Our only lucrative road game is against Kentucky; it is played on a so-called neutral court in Louisville, and each school makes about thirty thousand dollars. We'll let anybody boo us for that kind of money.

We also like to play in the major metropolitan areas like New York, Chicago, Los Angeles, and Philadelphia. They increase our media visibility and enable the greatest number of alumni and players' families to see us. Whether at home or away, we try to uphold our national image by playing teams from every part of the country. This season alone, we face representatives of nine major conferences: the Pacific-8, the Big Eight, the Big Ten, the Mid-American, the Missouri Valley, the Southeastern, the Southern, the Atlantic Coast, and the ECAC.

Finally, we prefer a difficult schedule because it helps sharpen us for tournaments. More than half our opponents had winning records last year, five of them finished in the Top 20, and two played in the final round of the NCAA tournament. We face four of the six most successful teams from the last five years, and seven of the top twenty-five from the last ten years. I do not know of a more difficult schedule in the country—and it starts in four days.

No wonder I haven't been sleeping well lately.

# WEDNESDAY, NOVEMBER 28

The coaches decide in their morning meeting that the day's practice schedule will cover the Ohio State game plan and include ten minutes of defensive preparation for Indiana. But the afternoon workout does not go as well as the coaches' three-by-five cards say it should. There are minor irritations: Shumate sprains a finger on his left hand, and still another Converse sneaker splits at the toe. But the biggest problem is the team's sluggishness.

"What's the matter?" Phelps asks Clay, his favorite barometer for gauging the team's mood.

"We're ready, coach," he says. "We need a game. It's been a long fall and we're anxious to get started."

Afterwards, the coaches decide to shorten the week's two remaining practices.

\*　\*　\*

I understand how the players feel, because it's the same for the coaches too. We've been waiting for this season to start since last March, and the final days are going by slowly.

I've been doing a lot of things to help pass the time. Terry and I went Christmas-shopping this morning, and our whole family had lunch with Fr. William Toohey's campus religious group. I also taped my first weekly television show with Tom Dennin on WNDU.

Despite today's emphasis on Ohio State and Indiana, we have not forgotten that our opening game is against Valparaiso. The Sunday after we play Valpo just does not give us enough time to get ready for the Buckeyes on Monday. And we will need every minute possible to prepare for a team as tough as Indiana.

A schedule like this is not unusual. We will concentrate on Valparaiso tomorrow and Friday, and our earlier drills for Ohio State and Indiana should help us on Saturday too.

Ara has a real advantage in playing only one opponent each week. No wonder he had time to send me a good-luck note today. And to think I used to write *him* letters.

## THURSDAY, NOVEMBER 29

Phelps has lunch at noon with representatives of Proctor & Gamble, who are interested in hiring Ken Wolbeck, a senior from Peoria, Illinois.

"What kind of security do you think he's after?," one of the men asks.

"The only security any graduate wants today is a job," Phelps answers, dusting off his Rider business degrees. "Look at the country's inconsistent economy and all the problems in Washington. Ken doesn't expect fifty thousand dollars a year and a lot of fringe benefits right away. He just wants a steady job with a good future."

\* \* \*

I'm sure this would be a good opportunity for Kenny, but I also know he would prefer to work for Caterpillar in his home town.

"Number one?"

"Notre Dame!"

"Number one?"

"Notre Dame!"

"Number one?"

"Notre Dame!"

Every Irish basketball practice ends with Phelps at center court raising a challenge and the players huddled around him giving their answer.

On this cold day in late November, the ritual has special significance. The seven weeks of preparation are over. Tomorrow at 2:00 P.M., the players and coaches begin trying to justify their "number one" claim.

None of them really believes Notre Dame will win the national championship, but to a man, they realize they can compete for it. "We'll be good this year," Clay says, summing up the general opinion. "We'll get a tournament bid, but I don't know what will happen after that."

Before the players shower, Phelps reminds them that their objective is, indeed, an NCAA tournament invitation. "We're about to start our third time-capsule," he says. "The first began the day you arrived on campus. We wanted you to play on your own and get to know each other. The second began with the start of practice. We've tried to prepare for the season by teaching you our system and by blending in the new personnel.

"Now the third time-capsule is about to begin. We must be ready to play a tough road schedule right away. Every player has to do his part to contribute to the success of the team. Hopefully, our experiences during the regular season will help get us through the NCAA tournament. That is the fourth time-capsule. We have come a long way in two years through hard work and dedication. This can be one of the greatest years in Notre Dame basketball history. Don't let me down."

Phelps then announces the starting lineup—which does, indeed, include Dantley—and goes through tomorrow's pre-game schedule. Mass will be said at 9:45 by Fr. Hesburgh. It will be followed by breakfast at 10:15. The players are on their own until 12:30, when they must report to the dressing room. DiBiaso, who is scouting Valparaiso's opening game tonight against Wisconsin-Oshkosh, will present his report an hour before the game.

At 1:20, Phelps will run through the game plan. Ten minutes later the players will begin warming up. They will return to the dressing room at 1:50 for Phelps' "psyching up" session and be back on the court at 1:55 for the introductions and two o'clock tip-off.

\* \* \*

I'm ready. We all are. After tomorrow, no more questions about how good we should be this year; people can judge for themselves. I was wondering about that myself tonight, when DiBiaso called after the Valparaiso game at about eleven o'clock.

"They won ninety-four to sixty-eight, but don't worry," he told me. "We will win tomorrow."

I hope so. It wouldn't be a very good start if we didn't.

## SATURDAY, DECEMBER 1

For Notre Dame fans, there has never been a premiere quite like this one. More than 11,000 enjoy a 112–62 romp —the largest opening-game explosion in the school's history.

The Irish are unsettled against the Crusaders at first, missing eight straight shots before Brokaw converts a driving lay-up with four minutes gone. By game's end, all fifteen uniformed players have scored and the team has made a dazzling 56 percent of its attempts from the floor. Starting in place of Crotty, Dantley leads the way with sixteen points and nine rebounds. Peter's first appearance comes at 12:20, but he takes only half a minute to can his first shot on a nice feed from Novak. Phelps gets his initial one-hundred-point game as Notre Dame coach when Drew hits his third straight basket with 5:57 remaining.

Dantley and Drew are not the only freshmen to stand out. Paterno misses only one of five shots, Knight hauls down seven rebounds, and Martin hands out seven assists. Frequent substituting limits the veterans' playing time, but Shumate still manages fifteen points.

The Irish are as pleased with their devastating performance as they are with the simple fact of having finally begun the season. "I don't have to score much in a game like this," Shumate says afterwards. "Digger was able to give everybody a chance to play, but it won't always be so easy."

In the Valparaiso dressing room, Coach Bill Purden begrudges the Irish nothing. "Notre Dame has a fabulous team with a good chance to go all the way," he says. He even suggests that with so much depth, Phelps' biggest problem could be keeping everyone happy.

Purden might easily be speaking of Crotty. "I'm more disappointed than anything else," Peter says. "After last year, it was kind of embarrassing not to start."

\* \* \*

I'm glad the first one is over. It relieved a lot of tension for everyone, though I will admit I would have been more nervous if we had opened against Michigan instead. They defeated us in our first game the last two seasons, so it feels good to start off with a win.

I hope playing well gave everyone plenty of confidence—especially the freshmen. Drew's impressive shooting against the zone should be useful against other teams later on.

It was good to see Peter come off the bench and do well. I considered starting the same five players as last year in order to recognize their NIT accomplishments, but Adrian's preseason performance could not be overlooked. I wanted to do what was best for the team *now* —this is a new season with new goals.

Later tonight I will watch Maryland play UCLA on television. There is a lot of talk about the strength of the Atlantic Coast Conference this year. That could be true, but I don't think Maryland has a chance in Pauley Pavilion. I should know what it's like—they've whipped us twice there. The ACC's best chance to beat UCLA will come in two weeks when North Carolina State plays the Bruins on a neutral court in St. Louis. If you want to know the truth, I'm hoping neither one of them stops UCLA. Ending that winning streak is a little pleasure we would like to have on January 19.

## SUNDAY, DECEMBER 2

Often during the school year Phelps invites the team to Sunday breakfast. As players and coaches sit around eating their stacks of pancakes this morning, they are as eager to talk about UCLA's game as their own.

The Bruins triumphed 65–64, but they gave Maryland a

chance to win in the last twenty seconds. The most frequently asked question is the one most difficult to answer: Are the Terrapins that good, or is UCLA finally vulnerable?

*　　*　　*

I couldn't be more surprised by last night's game, since I thought the officiating, the crowd, and UCLA's talent would be too much for Maryland. As it happened, the officiating was good, UCLA shot very poorly (less than 40 percent), and the Terrapins stayed in contention all the way. Their biggest break came when Keith Wilkes fouled out; in my opinion, he has always been the real key to the Bruin team.

This was an important game to watch, because we play UCLA twice this year, and we face Maryland next season. I had wondered how the Terrapins' sophomore guards would do, and I was impressed with how little trouble they had against UCLA's press. Maryland's biggest advantage seemed to be its size. Their big front line—which, fortunately for us, includes two seniors—hampered UCLA's shooting and gave them a lot of strength on the offensive boards. As small as we are, I don't know if we can do that.

The most encouraging thing was the surprisingly poor caliber of the Bruins' performance. This was not the same UCLA team I have seen in the past. Walton and Wilkes are still great, of course, but the other starters—Dave Meyers, Pete Trgovich, and Tommy Curtis—don't seem to have the same ability as some of their predecessors. I'm even more anxious now to watch them against North Carolina State, but not as anxious as I am to beat Ohio State tomorrow night.

## MONDAY, DECEMBER 3

Phelps never sends a team out to play without first giving the players some high purpose to consider. Basketball, he believes, is only 15 percent "doing it"; the other 85 percent is mental preparation.

His pregame talk is generally determined by the location of the game, its special significance, and the quality of the opposition. The alternate themes might be categorized "The Challenge Abroad/The Opportunity at Home," "An Important Game/A Big Game," and "We Will Win Unless . . ./ We Will Win If . . ." In effect, it's not unlike having dinner in a Chinese restaurant: two from Column A, one from Column B, and at half time Phelps has to feed them again.

On this evening in Columbus, Digger has a warning for the freshmen, who are playing before their first hostile crowd, and a challenge for the veterans, since this is their first rematch against an opponent that beat them last year.

"It won't be like last Saturday," he says. "This crowd is going to be on you the second you walk out the door. Just play your game, do what you can do, and don't let them bother you.

"December is an important month for us. We play four teams that beat us in close games last year. Ohio State is the first, so let's beat them tonight and worry about St. Louis, Indiana, and Kentucky later."

When the team returns at half time trailing 39–35, Phelps tries it again. "We didn't play good team defense and we didn't execute our offense," he says in the locker room. "You just weren't concentrating out there." Paterno knows Phelps is talking to him as much as anyone else. He missed five of his seven shots and drew a technical foul for throwing the ball inbounds to a surprised Novak after an Irish score.

"What in the world were you thinking about, Apple?" Phelps exclaims.

Notre Dame plays better in a tightly contested second half, but Ohio State seems to have the game won when Brokaw's fifth personal sends Wardell Jackson, the team's best foul-shooter, to the free-throw line with sixteen seconds left and the Buckeyes leading 67–65. Jackson misses the first shot of his one-and-one opportunity, and the Irish rebound. The seconds tick off as Clay moves quickly downcourt. He looks for Shumate inside, but sees a sagging defense instead. From twenty-one feet out and with seven seconds remaining, the Iceman shoots . . . and hits. Overtime.

After an exchange of baskets, Clay takes a pass from Shumate in the free-throw circle and breaks the game's fifteenth and final tie, putting the Irish ahead to stay. They win 76–72.

"A good win; we'll take whatever we can get," a relieved Phelps tells the team afterwards. A few minutes later the doors are opened to the members of the press, who are more interested in Clay's overtime-producing basket than Shumate's twenty-five points and seventeen rebounds. "It was the same kind of shot that beat Marquette last year," he explains. "I just prayed the ball would go in."

So, in fact, did all the Irish. Clay had made only two shots in ten attempts before hitting his shot at the buzzer.

\* \* \*

It was a lot closer than it should have been, but it's good to come home with a win. That is what really matters, especially since Ohio State is so tough to beat at home. We may have taken them too lightly; if so, it's my fault because my job is to get the team ready.

Dantley and Paterno were bothered by the crowd and the pressure, so I was hesitant to use the other freshmen. Hopefully, Ray, Toby, and the others learned by just watching, but I can't keep them out forever. To get that tournament bid, we've got to gamble with the young players. It may hurt us during the regular season as they gain experience, but in the long run it should pay off.

Even though Shumate and Brokaw played well and Dwight hit the key baskets, I am unhappy about our overall lack of concentration. Experienced players should execute plays better than ours did, although this could be a result of the long preseason. After seeing us play tonight, I think we would have been better off with an earlier start. We've lost some of the edge we had the last few days of practice.

After returning to South Bend, and finally getting to bed, I was awakened by a phone call about 1:30. It turned out to be a couple of fans in a Hazleton bar, who wanted to know the score of our game. When I hung up, Terry mumbled something about getting an unlisted phone number.

## TUESDAY, DECEMBER 4

Today, Peter Crotty is more sure than ever that his basketball career at Notre Dame has run aground. He played less against Ohio State than he has in any other college game, making one brief appearance with 5:26 remaining in the first half. During that 1 minute, 26 seconds he neither shot, scored, nor rebounded. His sole contribution: a personal foul.

"It really hurt my pride to sit there without being able to do anything," he says disappointedly. "I've been working hard in practice, yet I barely played at all. I guess it's going to be that way all year—Adrian starting and Apple coming off the bench. I hope not, but if it's that way, I'll have to accept it. I like Notre Dame too much to transfer. Maybe I've had my year to play, and now it's somebody else's turn."

Crotty says the indications have long been obvious. "I figured it would work out this way. The freshmen Digger recruited were just too good, and he knew all along the way things would develop."

*　*　*

I don't want Peter to give up on himself, because I haven't given up on him. He came into this season with thirty games under his belt, including some good performances against teams like Dayton, South Carolina, and Southern California. We need his experience.

Some people may have expected too much of Peter. Although he was the outstanding senior big man on Long Island his last year in high school, he will never be a dominant college player. That is nothing to be ashamed of, however. A lot of schools recruited him and would love to have him now. He's an unselfish player who never hurts us when he's in the game.

If Peter continues to work hard and make the proper adjustment from high school center to college forward, he could be a big help.

## WEDNESDAY, DECEMBER 5

Tomorrow's game with Northwestern has stirred more than the usual amount of interest in the Chicago newspapers. Notre Dame gets adequate coverage there anyway, but the prospect of two unbeaten teams playing in nearby Evanston is reason for special attention.

Occasions like this send Roger Valdiserri's sports information machinery into high gear. Releases must be written, statistics tabulated, interviews scheduled. Bob Best, a 1971 graduate seeking his masters in communication, is his assistant.

This has been a significant year for Valdiserri. As press liaison for the U.S. basketball squad which visited China this past summer, he observed a society totally dominated by the influence of one man. "Actually, it wasn't all that unfamiliar," he says. "We have much the same situation at Notre Dame with Ara."

But he is smiling as he says it.

\*    \*    \*

I respect Roger Valdiserri so much, it does not bother me at all that the cover of our press brochure shows Walton towering above Shumate as if he were about to block a shot. No, Roger and Shu have both assured me that John really scored on that play.

Actually, I can't imagine how we would survive without Roger's office. He does a super job of helping Notre Dame put its best foot forward. One of his most effective contributions is preparing players for interviews. A young athlete does not have enough experience with the press to always know how to handle himself. It is particularly difficult for our players, because we encourage them to fulfill interview requests whenever possible. Unlike some schools, we open our dressing room to the media after every game—win or lose, whether we feel like talking or not.

Roger does not tell the players what to say, but he does warn them about reporters who would manipulate them with misleading or negative questions. We have nothing to hide here, but we don't want our players in a position where they can unwittingly hurt themselves or the team. There are always a few reporters who are either anti–Notre Dame or who just want to knock somebody. So Roger advises the players to be careful and cooperative.

Some athletic teams post a saying in their locker room that goes, "What you see here and what you hear here, let it stay here when you leave here." If this means a player or coach should be uncooperative and secretive with the press, I disagree with it completely. But if it means there are occasional private matters that should not be publicly aired, then I would have to go along.

I consider my overall relationship with the press to be quite good. Reporters have generally been very fair to me and I have tried to be the same with them. I've taken my knocks, of course, especially following my decision to leave Fordham. Arthur Daley, a Fordham graduate, asked me to stay in a personal telegram, but later blasted me in his *New York Times* column. "Phelps," he wrote, "had broken a solemn contract, while Krause and Notre Dame at least were accessories after the facts and therefore guilty of complicity."

Pretty strong stuff, but Daley was not the only one. Eight months later, Milton Gross of the New York *Post* leveled two barrels at me—for holding the ball against UCLA and, once again, for leaving Fordham. "Digger left a lot of people unhappy," he wrote, "including the players he had recruited to play for him at Rose Hill. He had an obligation to those kids, which he pragmatically slighted, and he had an obligation to the NBC audience last Saturday and the spectators at the South Bend fieldhouse, who were short-counted."

Newspaper criticism must be as readily accepted as praise. My only objection in these instances was that neither man sought my side of the story. One of those considerate enough to give me that opportunity was Phil

Pepe of the New York *Daily News*. Two and a half weeks after Gross's column, Pepe wrote, "Couldn't they understand that this was what he always wanted? Couldn't they understand that a man must do what he thinks is right for himself, for his family? In return, he looked for understanding, too. It never came."

The country's sportswriters and sportscasters may write or say whatever they wish about a coach, and rightfully so. But I don't feel they are any more qualified to judge me than I am to accurately appraise them. For each of us there are complexities, demands, and techniques unknown and unappreciated by the other.

A good example of what I'm talking about (but by no means the only one) is the press commentary after our second UCLA game two years ago. Gross and others seemed to suggest that I had a greater obligation to the crowd and the television audience than I did to my own team. Coaches aren't entertainers; we don't devise our strategy to suit the spectators. In trying to run with UCLA earlier in the season, we had lost by fifty-eight points. I hoped that by holding the ball in the second game, we could keep down the margin and be within striking range when we picked up the tempo in the last ten minutes. It is always easier to come from behind at home, because the crowd is supporting us and we are more likely to get a break in the officiating. So we tried the stall and, needless to say, we lost again—this time by twenty-five points.

If the strategy was wrong, it was wrong because we lost, not because our style was dull. The more knowledgeable observers knew that if UCLA pressed us, instead of letting us hold the ball, we couldn't have used such an unpopular strategy in the first place. Nonetheless, no one criticized Wooden's strategy—because he won.

I realized long ago that very few basketball reporters fully understand the nuances of the game. When they stop writing human interest stories and try to become technical experts, they are over their heads. One of their more common mistakes is judging a player exclusively by his statistics. Too few reporters realize that the man scoring is no more important than his teammate who sets the screen. Or that the rebounder is no more essential than his teammate who blocks out. We practice these techniques constantly, but they never receive any publicity. Screens and blocks may be dull, but they are essential.

Nevertheless, I have great respect for the media. Their coverage of Notre Dame basketball is much appreciated for the recognition it brings and for the tickets it sells. We receive excellent support in South Bend from Woody Miller of the *Tribune,* Tom Dennin of WNDU, and Sam Smith of WSBT. Jack Lorri does our home games for WSJV in Elkhart. Regular coverage in Chicago comes from Dave Israel of the *Daily News,* Roy Damer of the *Tribune,* Bill Jauss of *Today,* and Bill Gleason of the *Sun-Times.* When I was at Fordham, I got to know such top New York writers as Gordon White and Sam Goldaper of the *Times,* Phil Pepe and Dave Hirshey of the *Daily News,* and Maury Allen and Dick Klayman of the *Post.*

I feel closest to the Philadelphia writers, because they gave me a thorough education in media relations. Frank Brady and Frank Bilovsky of the *Bulletin,* and Stan Hochman and Bill Conlin of the *Daily News,* were all that a freshman coach like me could handle. Another of that crew, *Inquirer* columnist Frank Dolson, became a close friend.

From a coach's point of view, there is one major difference between newspaper and television coverage—

a newspaperman, thank goodness, never interrupts a come-from-behind rally for a commercial time-out. Actually, any coach who wants his games televised must be willing to accept this as standard procedure. Television also affects scheduling. We agreed to change the date of one of our UCLA games this year from December 22 to January 26 in order to have it nationally televised. We consider ourselves very fortunate to be appearing on Eddie Einhorn's TVS network three times this season. We may not be number one in the wire service polls, but we're number one in the Nielsen ratings.

## THURSDAY, DECEMBER 6

Northwestern's opening-season victory streak of two games may be modest, but it is the team's longest since December 1966. After 11:23 of the first half against Notre Dame, the Wildcats seem capable of three in a row.

Northwestern is leading 25–19 when Phelps gathers his team for a time-out and orders a fullcourt press. Three minutes and ten points later, the Irish are ahead 29–27. With the quicker Martin in for Novak, Notre Dame's three-guard pressing attack forces four quick turnovers and sets up as many easy lay-ups. The Irish move out to a 49–37 half-time advantage and post a 98–74 victory. Dantley plays well, despite the muscle spasms in his back which have nagged him recently.

After talking to the press, showering, and dressing, the Notre Dame players board their chartered bus for the trip home. Digger, who wants to drive back with Terry and the

DiBiasos, leaves McLaughlin in charge. After letting off two Chicago friends, Phelps moves the blue-and-gold Thunderbird onto the Chicago Skyway toward South Bend. The conversation, of course, centers on the game. "The players gave us the defensive pressure we've been wanting," Digger says happily. "Ray did a good job in the press, and the big guys really pounded the boards."

"Yeah," says DiBiaso, sitting to his right. "We really spurted a couple of times, too. A steal, a quick basket, a steal, another basket."

The relaxed mood continues until the flashing lights of emergency vehicles come into view near the entrance to the Indiana Toll Road. "Is that our bus!" Phelps exclaims.

"I don't know, Digger," says DiBiaso, trying to see beyond the headlights. "It sure looks like it."

"Maybe it's Adrian's back," Phelps says, speeding to the scene. "Look! They're putting somebody into the ambulance."

Phelps brings the car to a screeching halt and jumps out into the cold night, only to be stopped by DiBiaso.

"Hey, Digger, move the car. It's right in the middle of the road."

Phelps pulls the car over and rushes to find Shumate, not Dantley, being helped into the ambulance.

"Frank!" he blurts out to McLaughlin. "What happened? What's wrong with Shu?"

McLaughlin hurriedly describes how Shumate had been standing up front, when the bus was suddenly sideswiped by a car it was passing. The bus driver swerved, causing Shumate to crash forward and tumble into the deep, narrow stairwell with his head jammed against the door. It was several minutes before Shumate's bulky 240 pounds could be extricated. For a while, McLaughlin tells Phelps, Shumate was unable to move the fingers of his right hand.

"Come on, Frank, let's ride over to the hospital," Phelps

says. "Dick, take Terry and Shawna to South Bend on the bus."

The coaches find a typically frustrating scene at the hospital emergency room. Even though Shumate complains of pain in his right shoulder, he is forced to stand in a long line for treatment. Preferring not to wait, Phelps gets permission to take Shumate to a hospital in South Bend. Shumate is uncomfortable during the eighty-minute drive, but after arriving at the hospital about 2:30, he has X rays taken which detect no broken bones.

A doctor diagnoses severe shoulder and rib bruises and lower back sprain. He recommends ice and heat treatments for the next thirty-six hours, and says, "Whether or not he plays Saturday will be up to him."

\* \* \*

John was very relieved to hear that his injuries were not serious. For that matter, we all were. As frightening as it was for us, when we first saw the bus on the side of the highway with police and ambulance lights flashing, I can imagine how much worse it was for Shu.

It would have been a terrible tragedy if he were seriously injured. After surviving that blood clot and infection as a sophomore, he has made remarkable progress—personally and athletically. Another setback would seem unfair.

Ironically, John is something of a hypochondriac. Nobody pays much attention when he takes a fall in practice or a game. Clay calls it his Redd Foxx act— you know, in "Sanford and Son" when Fred says, "It's a big one, Elizabeth. Here I come." They know that John is just catching his breath. Obviously, that was not the case tonight.

## FRIDAY, DECEMBER 7

Shumate feels better, but he is unable to participate in the preparation for St. Louis, a Missouri Valley Conference team which has won ten straight since last year. If Shu cannot play, Phelps has plans to move Novak to center and start Paterno or Crotty at forward.

\* \* \*

An amusing column in today's issue of the *Observer*, the student newspaper, suggests appropriate Christmas presents for various people. The writers came up with two I really like: a bearskin rug for Ara, and a copy of *They Call Me Digger* for John Wooden "when finished on January 19."

## SATURDAY, DECEMBER 8

Bruised and sore, Shumate decides to play against the Billikens anyway. His recovery and the lusty roars of the home crowd spark the Irish to an easy 94–65 victory. For once, Notre Dame takes command early as Shumate scores the first basket on a nice feed from Clay. Midway through the period, Shumate goes outside and launches a thirty-foot bomb that raises the score to 20–10. Everything works well for Notre Dame. In the first half alone, its press forces a staggering twenty-one turnovers and harasses the Billikens into 37 percent shooting.

The overwhelming victory adds to the festive mood at the

Phelpses' first open house of the year; the others will follow the Denver, UCLA, Duke, and Villanova games.

Although 150 people received invitations, Terry and Digger have learned to anticipate many more, especially after a victory. On this afternoon, much of the conversation over cocktails and hors d'oeuvres concerns the Sugar Bowl–bound football team. The big status symbols in South Bend these days are tickets to the game and confirmed room reservations at Notre Dame headquarters in the New Orleans Marriott.

When the last guest leaves shortly after seven o'clock, the three coaches go to McLaughlin's house on Rockne Drive to watch the Indiana-Kentucky game on television. The Irish play the Hoosiers on Tuesday, and the Wildcats on December 29.

Indiana's 77–68 victory is all the more impressive because it occurs in partisan Louisville.

"What do you think?" McLaughlin asks Phelps.

"I think," he says, "we've got a lot of work to do between now and Tuesday."

\* \* \*

Our game with Indiana is crucial for several reasons. They are one of the two or three best teams we face all season, and playing them in Bloomington only makes our job tougher. The Hoosiers are our biggest local rivals, and over the years, Notre Dame hasn't fared very well against them. Since the two schools began their rivalry in 1908, Indiana has won twenty-five of thirty-eight games, including the last three. Indiana is also the defending champion and current favorite in a conference we must compete with all the time—in games, recruiting, prestige, and media and fan attention. Finally, I have to admit that a little personal pride is involved.

Bobby Knight and I have an unspoken rivalry which

extends beyond the areas already mentioned. He is the best coach in the Big Ten, and one of the best in the country. I want my team to beat his. It is not unlike wanting to knock off the top gun in Dodge City; in coaching, the top guns are in places like Los Angeles, Milwaukee, Chapel Hill, and Columbia.

Despite our flecks of gray hair, the press often pairs us together as "bright young coaches." He is thirty-three and I am thirty-two, but the similarities go much further. We both started our head-coaching careers in New York—he at Army and I at Fordham. We both left New York in 1971 to come to Indiana. He has won the last two of our three games, but I am making a comeback—we lost by only two points last season, which was sixty-three better than the year before. Our 94–29 loss in 1971 came in the first game ever played at Assembly Hall, where Indiana's only defeat has been in double overtime. Finally, we are both intense coaches who emphasize aggressive defense.

## SUNDAY, DECEMBER 9

The coaches convene in Phelps' office at ten o'clock for two and a half hours of strategy-planning. Notre Dame has been preparing for this game off and on since before the season began. Now they must plot the afternoon practice schedule and finalize the game plan.

"They have good open shooters," says DiBiaso, who scouted Indiana's 72–59 victory over Kansas. "Their first seven players are all over fifty percent."

"We'll have to jam the ball," Phelps responds. "As soon as

they make a pass, we must have a defensive man right on top of the shooter."

"Knight is substituting quite a bit," adds DiBiaso. "You saw what Laskowski did last night when he came off the bench. What did he have, twenty-three points?"

"Yeah, I think that's what the paper said. . . . You know, we have better talent but Knight does a great job of making them concentrate on what he wants them to do. We need to emphasize three things with our own players: confidence, aggressiveness, and poise. That should help take their minds off the crowd. It's going to be even worse than it was at Ohio State. I hope the freshmen are ready for it."

The coaches break for lunch, returning in time for DiBiaso to give the prep team players their scouting assignments at 2:30. The regulars must be taped, dressed, and on the court by 3:00. Though Dantley's back is still bothering him, Shumate seems fully recovered and, during the next two hours, they engage in a spirited, enthusiastic workout.

Late in the afternoon, as the first team rehearses its fast break for the Indiana press, Brokaw is dribbling upcourt. Roger Anderson, on defense, swipes at the ball, causing a painful collision that sends both players sprawling. As practice stops, Anderson gets up, but Brokaw is unable to. When he finally does, he is barely able to walk. A doctor's examination shows severe contusions of the thigh, and he is ordered to stay overnight in the campus infirmary.

\* \* \*

All of a sudden, everything is going wrong. First Adrian, then Shu, now Gary. Shu was doing a lot better, but we had planned to have Adrian's back X-rayed tomorrow. Gene Paszkiet, the school's head trainer, came over tonight and said that Dantley's problem started in high school and that it is something he probably will always have to play with.

Gene also said that Gary's chances of playing Indiana are no better than 50–50. If there is any doubt, of course we won't use him. As much as we'd miss his outside shooting and his presence at midcourt in the press, Indiana is only one game. I'd rather see him recover fully and be ready for the rest of the season.

Right now, I'm very depressed and discouraged. This is a game we've worked very hard for, and nothing seems to be going right.

## MONDAY, DECEMBER 10

If Phelps is depressed, Brokaw is more so. He is the lone patient in a ward with a dozen beds. He has no television, no radio, and nothing to read. When Digger visits him, he solves one problem by asking the nurse to bring in a radio.

The bigger worry, Brokaw's injury, is not so easily eliminated.

"Will I play, coach?" he asks from his bed.

"We don't know yet," Phelps says.

Later in the day, the doctor makes his decision. Brokaw may neither play nor make the trip.

"But, Doc," pleads Gary. "At least let me see the game."

The doctor reconsiders, and when the team boards its Indiana Motor Bus after practice, Brokaw limps on with the help of crutches.

Once underway, the players tell Phelps they would prefer a bag full of Burger Chef cheeseburgers to a restaurant meal. Thus fortified, and entertained by Shumate's ever-present tape player, the team arrives at the Holiday Inn outside Bloomington about midnight. As they unload, somebody notices the familiar marquee. "Welcome Notre Dame," it says on one side.

And on the other, a message that more clearly indicates local opinion. "Go Big Red."

* * *

The ride to Bloomington was nice and relaxing. As Frank said, at least we weren't run off the road again. It was good to have Gary along, even though he won't be playing. And when I saw John off in a corner content with his tape player, *I* was even inspired with a little confidence.

We've decided to move Clay to Brokaw's number-two wing-guard position and fill the number-one point-guard spot with Martin. Ray has been playing the good defense we expected of him all along, and he has been a pleasant surprise on offense. Still, we would be better off with Brokaw's experience.

## TUESDAY, DECEMBER 11

Tonight's game is given added significance by the week's new Associated Press poll, which shows Indiana still in third place and Notre Dame up two notches to sixth.

Following a 10:30 breakfast, the team rides to Assembly Hall for an hour of light shooting. Misfortune strikes again, however, when Shumate sprains the middle finger of his left hand.

Back at the motel, Phelps shows the team the final reel of last season's Indiana game film. "When you get out there tonight," he tells the players, "I want you to remember what happened last year. We had a fifty-one to thirty-eight lead with twelve minutes to go, and blew it. We can't let that happen again."

During the pregame Mass, Fr. Jim Shilts makes a brief reference to the disastrous 1971 Indiana game which is lost on every player except Novak. Shumate sits quietly, but he suddenly interrupts the informal service by loudly calling out to the trainer, "Arno, my finger's turning blue."

Phelps reacts even more quickly than Zoske. "John, just take the tape off," he says.

When next seen, Shumate is sitting in the restaurant eating his pregame meal with his left hand wrapped in ice.

Shortly after 6:00 P.M., the team loads up for the short trip to Assembly Hall. Even as they file through the players' entrance, a record-breaking 17,463 fans are filling the arena. The minuscule Irish rooting section is comprised of Chicago lawyer and Notre Dame graduate Ed O'Rourke, who has been following the basketball team for years. The football banquet being held tonight in South Bend has kept even the cheerleaders away.

"How about Terry?" somebody asks Phelps. "Where is she?"

"She had an exam today," Digger says.

"Ah," teases DiBiaso. "I'd rather have Austin Carr here anyway."

"I called Terry a while ago," Phelps continues. "She said Rick was so nervous about the game he didn't want to sing in school."

Loud music by the Doobie Brothers fills the dressing room as the players go about their pregame rituals. Novak and Martin have their ankles taped. Clay stretches stomach-down on the training table so Arno Zoske can give his legs a massage. Shumate pulls a flesh-colored support stocking over his left leg. Dantley stretches the powerful muscles in his arms and upper torso.

After the players have dressed and Phelps has finished scribbling the offensive and defensive strategy on a blackboard, everyone gathers for the pregame talk.

"Jam the ball," he tells them. "Don't let them take open shots. And no turnovers against their press. You're better than this team. When you go out there, forget about the crowd and the referees and everybody else. Just beat them with your talent. Ray, if you can play people like Nate Archibald on the playground, you shouldn't have any trouble with a bunch of college kids.

"Indiana is third in the country and we're sixth," he continues. "After we beat them tonight, and if UCLA beats North Carolina State on Saturday, we'll move up to number two. And that's how it will stay until we play UCLA in January. Then we'll be number one."

Phelps, it seems, perceives a grand design unrealized by the players.

When the team leaves to warm up, Brokaw goes with them, but he doesn't stay very long.

"I can't take that, man," he says, bounding in on his crutches. "Not playing really hurts."

The other players return in twenty minutes for their final instructions. "Let's have five minutes of intensity at the start," Phelps orders. "Really go after them. We got revenge against Ohio State and St. Louis. Now, let's beat Indiana."

A huddle, a prayer, a clap, a cheer, and they are gone.

When Phelps meets Knight in front of the scorer's table to exchange pregame pleasantries, he is wearing a wide grin that seems to say, "This is it. I know just how you feel."

The play of both teams is ragged at the start, but Digger gets the five-minute burst of intensity he ordered, almost to the second. After Notre Dame hounds Indiana into a half-dozen turnovers and takes a 9–4 lead, Knight calls time out.

It remains a frustrating half for the Hoosiers, who outshoot the Irish from the field and commit fewer turnovers, but still trail at the end 33–30. Notre Dame's advantage is built on superior free-throw shooting and rebounding, and on Shumate's total domination of both Indiana centers, 6′ 7″ sophomore starter Tom Abernethy and heralded 6′ 10″ freshman Kent Benson.

Through the entire twenty minutes, Indiana never leads. Six times, the Hoosiers tantalize the crowd by cutting the Irish advantage to one, only to have Notre Dame pull away again. Significantly, five of the answering Irish baskets are put in by freshmen Dantley and Paterno.

At intermission, Phelps criticizes such indiscretions as the team's seventeen turnovers, and he reminds them of Indiana's second-half aggressiveness against Kentucky. "You outplayed 'em," he says. "Now beat 'em."

Through most of the second half, Notre Dame seems capable of nothing less. For the fourth and fifth times in the game, forward Steve Green scores to pull Indiana within one, but the go-ahead points refuse to come. With twenty-four seconds left, an official's call sends Clay to the free-throw line and the crowd into a frenzy. Knight is incensed, as the fans chant "Bullshit!" and pelt the court with debris that strikes Shumate and Paterno. He tells the officials to call a technical foul on his own team if the display continues.

When play resumes, the Iceman ices another game. Clay sinks two free throws to make the score 72–67, and Shumate hits his twenty-sixth point of the evening to seal a 73–67 victory that stops Indiana's home winning-streak at nineteen games.

Moments later the Irish dressing room is in pandemonium. Phelps embraces Novak and shouts to no one in particular, "To win down here is like beating the world!" A few feet away, Shumate is caught in the middle of a back-slapping assault. Brokaw holds his crutches triumphantly aloft as he hops around on one foot.

Elsewhere, a somber Knight contrasts the Irish mood. "Notre Dame deserved to win," he says. "From the first minute to the last, there was not one moment where we played with the determination they did. The difference was their intensity and the way Dantley and Shumate handled us on the backboards. Those two really pounded us."

Meanwhile, Phelps is telling Bob Best to have a welcome ready for the Irish when they arrive at about one o'clock. Before leaving the hall, he stops to chat with the Hoosier's Benson, the state's "Mr. Basketball" last year, whom he had tried unsuccessfully to recruit. The tall freshman confides that the adjustment to college ball has been difficult. Phelps understands, but he knows also that it was Notre Dame's freshmen who were the unexpected difference for his own team. Dantley played all forty minutes and finished with fifteen points, thirteen rebounds, and six assists. Martin responded well in his first starting role, despite losing a sneaker in the first half and receiving a technical foul in the second. And Paterno came off the bench to play all but six and a half minutes and total sixteen points and six rebounds.

\* \* \*

It's unbelievable that we won without Brokaw; the freshmen were the difference. Credit their high school coaches for this one: Morgan Wootten (Adrian), Jim Gatto (Ray), and Vinnie Cox (Bill). If these kids can survive pressure like this, they should be all right the rest of the season. They've made a lot of progress since the Ohio State game, and the team has come right along with them.

As we rode back to South Bend, I couldn't help recalling a scene after the Indiana loss two years ago. After we stopped for dinner in a nice restaurant, one of the players said, "Coach, we don't deserve this." To show how times have changed, tonight we left Bloomington with a victory, eating dinner out of a cardboard box.

When we finally pulled onto campus about 1:30, we were greeted by two to three hundred students. I don't know how Bob Best managed to get that many out in 24° weather, but we sure appreciated the welcome. Even Fr. Joyce was there. I said a few words to everyone about how happy we were to win, and then Goose and Shu spoke. Some of the students wanted to hear from the freshmen too, but I thought they should wait a while—until they are juniors or seniors.

It was nearly two o'clock when I walked into the house. Terry had cooled some champagne in the refrigerator, but I was too tired to enjoy it. Instead, I drank a quick bourbon and ginger ale and went to bed. But I didn't fall asleep until after three. As happy as I was to have won, I couldn't help but worry about the long season ahead. It's going to take a lot more wins like this one to get a bid.

## WEDNESDAY, DECEMBER 12

A coach's analytic approach to basketball is evident in the morning meeting. While assessing last night's game, DiBiaso speaks in the mystical cant that only another X-and-O'er could understand: "When number one was forced out of his normal entry, number two wasn't coming back to help." Translation: Clay was not making himself available to receive a pass when Martin got into trouble bringing the ball upcourt.

Phelps makes notes as DiBiaso points out other vulnerable areas which need attention in practice, and which might be exploited if the two teams played again. Among them are the necessities to box out better when rebounding and to make fewer crosscourt passes against the press.

At 11:30, Phelps rides over to the WNDU television studio to tape his Saturday show. The host is Tom Dennin, who also does the radio affiliate's play-by-play description. Despite being a university-owned station, WNDU does not have exclusive rights to the game broadcasts. It has a less-powerful signal than WSBT which, so the story goes, received its own broadcasting rights after Johnny Dee's wife once noticed that WNDU could not be heard outside South Bend.

Phelps' guest this week is Shumate, who arrives fifteen minutes late wearing his characteristic wide grin and wider-brimmed fedora. The three take their seats on a lifeless living-room set which, curiously, suggests neither Notre Dame nor basketball. Phelps is irritated by the show's lack of planning and organization, but not enough so to ask for better. Certainly it seems unusual that films of last year's NIT are still being shown four games into the 1974 season.

The taping is saved by Dennin's relaxed, professional manner and Shumate's ebullient personality, which can provoke a smile even when none is intended.

"My main reason for being in school is to get an education," he says. "But I'm a city ball player, too. I'm not going to say I spend *all* my time studying."

When Dennin asks Shumate about the performances of his young teammates against Indiana, John answers, "I wasn't leery of the freshmen, but I did wonder if they would be able to hold up under a crowd that would be on them every minute of the game."

Later that afternoon, a salesman for Pro-Keds basketball shoes calls on Phelps. The visit seems less than coincidental, since last night's television broadcast showed Martin slipping and sliding early in the game after losing one of his Converse low-cuts. "When that happened, I was really burned," says Digger. "You'd think somebody could make a shoe that stayed on and stayed together."

Phelps orders sample pairs of high- and low-cuts for each player. "I'll let the kids decide," he tells the man. "If they like your shoe better, we will use them too."

The salesman, smelling a deal, takes his leave.

\* \* \*

The heavy competition among the shoe manufacturers is a situation I prefer to ignore. We wore Adidas last year and then changed to Converse, because I liked the way their green suede looked. I really don't care, as long as the shoe looks nice, wears well, and is liked by the players.

Apparently our win had quite an impact, because the phone nearly rang off the hook today. Writers and sportscasters were calling from everywhere. I was free to talk, since we weren't practicing.

## THURSDAY, DECEMBER 13– SATURDAY, DECEMBER 15

With final exams near and just two games remaining in December, Notre Dame's only workout after Indiana is held on Friday.

On Saturday afternoon, Phelps takes Rick to a circus in the always-bustling Athletic and Convocation Center. Afterwards, he settles in front of his television to watch the long-anticipated game between UCLA and North Carolina State. Although both were undefeated last year, they could not play each other in the NCAA tournament. The Atlantic Coast Conference champions were ineligible because of recruiting violations involving their two biggest stars, David Thompson and Tommy Burleson.

* * *

Watching UCLA tear apart North Carolina State 84–66 on a neutral court, with Bill Walton on the bench for half the game, was a sobering experience. After a while, I recovered enough to make notes for our bulging UCLA file:

1. The keys to the game were Keith Wilkes' defensive job on David Thompson, and his ability to turn on offensively after Walton got into foul trouble. Wilkes, not Walton, will be our toughest defensive assignment. (I write Walton off as unstoppable.)

2. UCLA stayed close in the first half because of its rebounding. (The Bruins are big and aggressive.)

3. North Carolina State led early because it was willing to attack Walton. (This is my philosophy exactly.)

4. UCLA has tremendous depth at center, with Drollinger and Washington playing behind Walton. (We don't.)

5. UCLA wore down State with its superior depth at forward and guard. (Fortunately, we have depth at these positions.)

6. UCLA's press forced North Carolina State to hurry down the floor and rush its shots. (We should not be forced into that unless we can find a high-percentage shot.)

7. N.C. State stayed in contention as long as it showed poise and patience; it lost both—and the game

—when Walton returned. (Poise and patience will be keys for us.)

It was great for college basketball to have a game that generated so much attention and excitement. I think the spectators liked it even when Walton came on so strongly in the last ten minutes to blow State out.

By playing UCLA at home, we could have an exciting game and, perhaps, an opportunity to win. Apparently, I'm not the only one around here thinking about it, either. A student called this evening to ask if we were interested in having a pep rally the night before we play. I told him there is one already planned.

Later, at a Christmas party for English graduate students and teachers, I met Professor Don Gutierrez, who is a UCLA alumnus. He told me he has been getting a lot of ribbing lately, but I don't guess I was too sympathetic. I hope he understood.

The party was especially enjoyable because it gave me a chance to know some of our faculty members better. Terry always speaks well of her professors, and I was pleased to find them interested in athletics. This creates a good environment for a coach to work in.


## SUNDAY, DECEMBER 16

Phelps' five-game unbeaten streak comes to an end today—all for a good cause. For the second year in a row, he limbers up his flaccid playing muscles and joins some other adults in a charity game against students from Logan Center, the St. Joseph County school for the mentally retarded. Phelps' team takes a fourteen-point lead, falls behind, ties the score, goes ahead by four, and then loses. The best indication that the outcome may have been fixed is that Digger never yells at anybody.

*　*　*

The game today was a lot of fun—much more fun, I might add, than the sloppy practice the Notre Dame team had later. I have been the honorary chairman for the Logan Center fund-raising drive the last two years. Getting involved in something like this really helps a person straighten out his values. It makes me realize I have things pretty easy compared to a lot of people.

## MONDAY, DECEMBER 17

Tempers are short and elbows swift in today's scrimmage, making the area underneath the basket a no-man's land. The irritation may be due to tensions built up during examinations, or to the boredom brought on by this lull in the schedule. Whatever the cause, for every shot fired from outside, two bodies fall in the rebound scuffling inside. In one skirmish, Shumate pushes Crotty, who had elbowed Clay. "I didn't mean it," Peter says to Dwight. No other words are spoken and no more apologies offered, but the glares are hard and cold.

That night, Crotty is still steaming about the incident in his dorm room when the phone rings.

"Hey, Crotty, this is Shu."

"Yeah?"

"Look, man, I just wanted to apologize for getting into it with you in practice. Okay?"

"Yeah, Shu, thanks. Look, it was my fault too."

"So, it's all forgotten then?"

"Yeah. And, listen, I really appreciate it."

\* \* \*

There are worse ways for players to let off steam, so a little bit of temperament isn't too bad. But they know that I won't tolerate its getting out of hand. Overall, I think it was a profitable afternoon's work: we prepared for Denver, and we worked on our offenses against Kentucky's 1-3-1 halfcourt zone trap and zone defense.

After practice, Roger Valdiserri and I joined students, faculty, and administrators at a Christmas buffet in Stepan Center. These affairs are important because they let all of us get to know each other's problems better. People have to appreciate what you are doing before they are willing to get behind you.

I picked up Ray Martin on the way home because he wanted to show Terry a paper he had written. Terry told him she was very impressed, which was encouraging to both of us. It's still touch and go for several players academically, especially Adrian. Getting ready for Denver won't be easy, with so many of them missing practice because of exams.

# TUESDAY, DECEMBER 18

Notre Dame's advancement in the latest weekly poll falls short of the prediction Phelps made before the Indiana game. The Wolfpack and the Hoosiers have fallen to fifth and seventh places, but the spot behind UCLA has been awarded to Maryland. Notre Dame must be content with third.

\* \* \*

Actually, I am quite happy with being third, as long as we have the chance to go higher. I didn't really think we could jump from sixth to second; the polls just don't work that way. But I wanted the players to believe in themselves to the extent they *thought* it was possible. Everyone knows that the only ranking which means anything is the one a team determines for itself in the NCAA tournament. Although I follow the weekly ratings as closely as anyone—and sometimes curse them just as loudly—I recognize that their real importance is their psychological value.

An opponent ranked above us offers an opportunity to advance. Any team ranked below us, or better yet, any unranked team, is the "villain" trying to knock us off. Either way, it challenges the team's pride.

The toughest thing about national ranking is not winning it, but keeping it. I remember the thrill we had at Fordham after making the Top 20 and the mounting excitement as we climbed higher. At Notre Dame, it's different because we began the year in the Top 10. People expect us to win and, in a certain way, so do we.

Unfortunately, the public believes the best teams should win every game. If this is true, it is true only of UCLA. The Bruins have accomplished what no sports team ever has before: they have made winning completely routine and absolutely predictable. Every coach who plays UCLA tells his team pretty much the same thing: "They can't win forever. They have to lose sometime. Maybe this is the game. Accept the challenge. Imagine the opportunity. Consider the consequences."

All of that feeling is dramatized in the weekly wire-service polls. The AP selections are made by the media, and the UPI choices by a coaches' panel, of which I am a member. In case you're wondering, this week I voted us third, with North Carolina second.

## WEDNESDAY, DECEMBER 19

Denver, tomorrow's opponent, is one of two challenges Phelps and his staff face this week. The other is the mountain of envelopes balancing precariously on each desk. No one knows for sure but, at last count, the Notre Dame coaches had a Christmas card mailing-list with more than seven hundred names. It's enough to give even the jolliest Santa a case of writer's cramp.

\* \* \*

Christmas cards are about the only way I can keep in touch with all my former players. I try to send one to each of them—a tradition that could force me out of coaching in ten years.

## THURSDAY, DECEMBER 20

Gary Novak's three baskets and one assist lead an early burst against Denver which gives Notre Dame a 10–2 lead. The outcome is all but decided when the half ends 52–30.

After observing a 99–59 Irish romp which produces seventeen more rebounds, eleven more assists, fifteen fewer turnovers, and 55 percent shooting, Denver coach Al Harden laments, "They didn't look sharp, but they still beat us by forty points."

\* \* \*

We were sloppy tonight, and our reserves made very poor use of their playing time. After taking an 80–38 lead, we were outscored 21–19. Nevertheless, I think Crotty may be able to help us against Kentucky. The most encouraging part of the game was our ability to score against their zone. We may be zoned a lot this year.

## FRIDAY, DECEMBER 21

The players head home for a well-deserved five-day vacation, with more to celebrate than the team's 6–0 record. Despite all the apprehension and foreshadowings of doom, the academic battle has been won. It was a close finish for some but, with Mike DeCicco's help, every freshman came in above the required 1.75 cumulative average. Dantley even pulled a *C* in physics.

## SATURDAY, DECEMBER 22

With his team scattered across the country and McLaughlin away scouting Kentucky, there is not much for the head basketball coach to do. The home front is just as quiet—Terry is running errands with Jennifer, and Karen is taking ballet lessons. The two dogs, Spanky and Schultz, are sleeping.

"C'mon, Rick," Phelps says. "We're going to football practice."

Because South Bend is under a blanket of snow, the football team has moved inside the ACC. Soon after they arrive, Rick stations himself beside quarterback Tom Clements in the offensive huddle. Minutes later, he scrambles up a small tower normally reserved for Parseghian and proceeds to solve an assortment of wishbone defensive problems which heretofore completely baffled the combined genius of the Irish staff.

\* \* \*

Rick is smart. He knows football coaches make more money than we do and don't work at night.

## SUNDAY, DECEMBER 23

This evening Phelps finishes reading *UCLA Basketball: The Real Story,* a critique of John Wooden's program, tactics, and philosophy. By now, Phelps' copy might pass for the annotated version. It is profusely marked with underlined passages and margined comments, all of which will be transcribed by Mrs. Van Paris for distribution to DiBiaso and McLaughlin.

* * *

I feel a little bit like Patton reading a biography of General Rommel. I much prefer this book to John's less revealing autobiography, *They Call Me Coach*.

This particular book gives me new insights into Wooden and confirms some others I have always had. For instance, it points out that he is more a practice coach than a game coach because he does not like to make adjustments. With this in mind, we hope to create situations which make UCLA lose its composure.

Another point concerns the Bruins' press. Its importance is not the turnovers it causes, but the way it forces a faster tempo and makes a team play offense on both ends of the court. Wooden does not like an opponent to come downcourt easily and set up where it wants to.

I've also been thinking about UCLA's personnel. To stop the lob pass, Shumate should play behind Walton this year instead of fronting him. When Walton gets the ball, we'll have to force him into the middle and make him pass off. Shu is as strong as Walton, so he should be able to go one-on-one with him, and maybe even get him into foul trouble.

I don't think their wing men, Meyers and Trgovich, are as good as the Farmers and Hollyfields they've had in the past. They don't run, shoot, or press as well. In my opinion, Brokaw and Dantley are better. Curtis and Clay are a fairly even match-up, though I wish Dwight would be as spirited and fiery as Tommy. Of course

Wilkes is superior to Novak, but there are few forwards anywhere as good as he is.

My early impression is that we have a good chance of beating them this year, especially at home.

## MONDAY, DECEMBER 24

Christmas Eve is strictly business for Notre Dame's coaching staff. In a two-and-a-half-hour meeting, McLaughlin assesses Kentucky, which won its annual invitational tournament this weekend by defeating Dartmouth and Stanford.

"They have very good speed," McLaughlin says. "They all shoot and handle the ball well and, defensively, they are pressing more often."

McLaughlin adds that the Wildcats' lack of size—center Bob Guyette is only 6' 8"—should give Notre Dame a distinct rebounding advantage.

"Then we should work on our zone offense," Phelps says. "They can't match up with us man-to-man, so they will probably have to zone some. We can go to our power game, looking to penetrate and control the boards. What about our defense?"

"They won't be as easy to press as some other teams," McLaughlin says. "They're so small, it's like playing against four guards and a forward."

Phelps spends the afternoon viewing the Indiana game film, listing thirteen ways Notre Dame can either improve its own weaknesses or capitalize on Indiana's. He already anticipates the Hoosiers' winning the Big Ten title and playing Notre Dame in the Mideast Regional.

*  *  *

Sitting at home tonight, I felt kind of homesick. I told Terry I wished we had a private plane so I could fly to New York, spend a few hours with my parents, and be back here by morning to watch the children open presents.

I hope my own kids feel the same affection for their home when they grow older. Right now, all they can think about is Santa Claus. Jennifer is really juiced; she's been yelling and fighting with her brother and sister and has been quite a handful.

It also occurred to me how different Frank's life is from mine and Dick's. I wonder if being away from his family makes him lonely? I'm sure he will get married eventually, but if he doesn't, he will probably continue to be one of the happiest bachelors in the world.

## TUESDAY, DECEMBER 25

Santa Claus has come to town, leaving a trail of tattered wrapping paper, unstrung ribbons, and toys already in need of repair. When Digger calls his parents in Beacon, he learns that Santa's bag has even included a present for the team.

"Merry Christmas and congratulations," his father says.

"For what?"

"Haven't you seen the morning paper? You're now up to second place in the UPI poll."

Later in the afternoon, Digger and Terry stop by a friend's house for cocktails and return home to welcome Frank for

Christmas dinner. Afterwards, Dick and Shawna join them for dessert, an exchange of gifts, and reminiscences about the less-prosperous days of the nation's number two basketball team.

*　*　*

I had a very mixed reaction to the ranking. I didn't want us to be that high until after the Kentucky game. Now the pressure is really on. If Kentucky upsets us, it will make their season and ruin the momentum I wanted us to build for the UCLA game. Nevertheless, it was a Merry Christmas.

## WEDNESDAY, DECEMBER 26

Although the student body is not due on campus until January 15, the basketball team must report back today. When everyone assembles for a screening of the Indiana film, one player—Dwight Clay—is nowhere to be found. Nor does he appear during an hour-and-a-half workout in the auxiliary gym. There is still no sign of him when the team moves upstairs for a scrimmage in the main arena. At 10:00 P.M., thirty minutes before the end of practice, Clay finally appears.

"Where have you been, Dwight?" Phelps asks in a less-than-pleased tone of voice.

"Plane connection problems, Digger. Sorry."

*　*　*

I'm in no mood for problems of any kind. Until we play UCLA, in fact, I'll probably be in a very bad mood.

## THURSDAY, DECEMBER 27

More problems. A shooting practice is scheduled for 11:00 A.M. At 11:15 Clay, Brokaw, Knight, and Martin are missing. Phelps tells the manager, John Palkovics, to call the Morris Inn, where the players are staying while their dormitories are closed. Palkovics' call awakens all four, and it is 11:45 before they arrive at the ACC. At 11:46 Phelps orders everyone to the locker room, where he does a very good imitation of an exploding bomb.

\*    \*    \*

Shumate told Terry that he has never seen me as mad as I was this morning. He's probably right. We're playing Kentucky in two days, and I've got four Sleeping Beauties on my team. Tomorrow, they will probably want breakfast in bed. With classes out and the campus deserted, the players should be working at basketball harder than ever.

My message must have gotten through, because everyone showed up on time for the afternoon practice.

## FRIDAY, DECEMBER 28

Phelps' schedule for today is an orderly list of family and business chores: 7:30—Get up; eat breakfast; pack for a ten-day trip to Louisville, New Orleans, and Fort Lauderdale. 9:00—Take Rick to the barbershop. 10:00—Basketball practice. 1:30—Join the six-car caravan headed for Louisville.

Unfortunately, nothing works out as planned.

The private plane which will fly them from Louisville to New Orleans has a two-suitcase limit—hardly sufficient for five people visiting three cities in ten days. The trip to the barbershop becomes an emergency dash to the hospital when Rick closes the car door on his thumb. Five stitches and "Don't go near the water."

Because of the accident, Digger is the last to arrive at practice. Later, as the 1:15 deadline for meeting the team passes, Phelps is missing again. While others watch and wait, Digger and Terry discuss in husband-and-wife fashion why they are late—which is to say, they argue.

When the five Phelpses finally arrive at the Morris Inn, Digger takes some heavy ribbing from his players. Clay doesn't say much. He just smiles.

After a long drive, interrupted by a stop at the Dairy Queen outside Kokomo, Indiana, the Notre Dame team arrives in Louisville.

As the players get out of the cars, Bill Paterno looks around, puzzled.

"What's the matter, Apple?" somebody asks.

"I can't understand it," the New Jersey boy says seriously. "Where's all that blue grass I've heard about?"

\* \* \*

This day certainly had its problems. It's been especially rough on Terry lately, since she has had to worry about passing her exams and getting ready for the holidays. Now she must look after the kids and put up with me while we prepare for Kentucky. It will be easier when we get to Florida. I'll just prop her up in a chair and fly her back in time to start the second semester.

# SATURDAY, DECEMBER 29

In the twelve years since Kentucky and Notre Dame began their December series in Louisville's Freedom Hall, the Irish have counted their wins at the box office and their losses—ten of them—on the court. It is a colorful, if one-sided, rivalry marked by large crowds, high scores and, in three of the last four meetings, close finishes. Nor is it without occasional controversy. Johnny Dee once refused to play unless some ball besides an "Adolf Rupp" autographed model were used.

On this particular evening, Notre Dame's size and strength are too much for the Wildcats. Kentucky coach Joe Hall starts 6' 10" Roger Wood instead of Guyette at center. But after the sophomore picks up three fouls in less than six and a half minutes, he is waved permanently to the bench.

Notre Dame builds a 43–35 half-time lead on balanced scoring and strong rebounding by Novak, Dantley, and Shumate. A 12–4 spurt at the start of the second half breaks the game open, but Phelps is reluctant to substitute against the faster, quicker Wildcats. Digger sticks with the regulars as the Irish bull their way to a 94–79 victory. It is a masterful performance after such a long lay-off. Notre Dame makes 58 percent of its shots from the field, eighteen of twenty-two from the free-throw line, and out-rebounds the Wildcats 40–24.

Afterwards, Jimmy Dan Conner of Kentucky says Notre Dame is "about the same as Indiana and a shade behind North Carolina." Then he adds, "But I think they've got a shot at UCLA, I really do."

\* \* \*

I can relax a little now. When we play UCLA we should still be unbeaten, because I don't think Xavier and Georgetown can upset us at home.

After the game I went back to the motel, where I ate a couple of sandwiches and watched the replay of the game on television. I enjoyed every minute of it.

Two years ago, after Kentucky beat us 83–67, I was sitting in this same motel just thankful it hadn't been worse, when Coach Rupp called. "Coach," he said, "about three or four people have asked me why we didn't beat you the way Indiana and UCLA did. I was sort of wondering the same thing myself. We had a thirty-point lead and only won by sixteen." All I could think to say was that our press worked better after he took Ronnie Lyons out of the game. Rupp was very nice and didn't seem upset, but I think now his call was prompted by the people trying to make him retire.

The only call I got after tonight's game was from some bigot who wanted to know why I played so many blacks. Only he used a different word.

## SUNDAY, DECEMBER 30

The Phelps family gets up early to catch that free flight to New Orleans, courtesy of Robert Levy, a Philadelphia businessman Digger has known since his days at Penn. Also on board are McLaughlin; a friend from New York, Vinnie Russo; and Fr. James Riehle, who schedules the priests for the team Masses.

The scene at the Marriott Hotel is typical of the entire French Quarter during Sugar Bowl week: crowds, congestion, noise, and celebration. "If I were Ara," Phelps tells McLaughlin, "I'd want to stay someplace else. This is unbelievable."

While Terry takes the kids out for a boat ride on the Mississippi, Phelps, McLaughlin, and Russo head for a high school game in Baton Rouge. Like a half-dozen other coaches in the stands, they are interested in 6' 10" Rick Robey, a well-regarded center from Brother Martin High in New Orleans. Unfortunately, they arrive just in time to see Robey foul out in the second half.

"What a waste of time," Phelps complains.

"Yeah," says McLaughlin, pointing out Kentucky coach Joe Hall, who sits nearby, "but how do you think he feels today?"

Later that evening, Digger and Terry feast on boeuf Wellington in an excellent French restaurant, Louis XVI.

"You should have seen Rick today," Terry says over tea. "Every time he saw somebody wearing a red hat, he said, 'There goes an Alabum.'"

*　*　*

It looks like most of South Bend made it to New Orleans. The students have overrun the place, including Novak, Crotty, and Wolbeck, whom we ran into on Bourbon Street about 1:00 A.M.

I saw Ara only briefly, just long enough to shake his hand and wish him luck. He's probably a little tense right now, hoping the team is ready for anything, and wanting every player to be completely aware of his assignment. I don't think it bothers him that Alabama is favored. This means he has everything to win and nothing to lose.

Here's my Sugar Bowl prediction: If we play them even in the first half and don't fall too far behind, we will win. Bob Thomas, our field-goal kicker, should be the key because it's going to be a very close game.

# MONDAY, DECEMBER 31

Phelps' last day of 1973 is an epicure's delight. First he eats breakfast with Philadelphia columnist Frank Dolson, followed by brunch at Brennan's with Terry. Then it's on to lunch with Rick Robey's parents, and finally, a pregame buffet hosted by Fr. Joyce.

Part of the conversation at brunch centers on Jason Miller, the celebrated author of Broadway's *That Championship Season,* who played in *The Exorcist.* Miller, it turns out, is in New Orleans to write about the Sugar Bowl.

"Roger Valdiserri introduced Terry and me to him this morning," Phelps says. "We saw his play last March when we were in New York for the NIT. It reminded me a little of my team in Hazleton, since the team in the play also won the Pennsylvania state championship. We've already had one reunion, and I can imagine our meeting again in twenty years. I don't expect any problems like the ones he wrote about, but I do think there were a few similarities between his characters and some of the kids on my team."

Phelps and the Robeys are hosted at lunch by Herb Bernstein, Mr. Robey's employer and a contractor in New Orleans. Phelps shows only cautious interest in Rick, because he must evaluate other big men before formally offering a scholarship.

Afterwards, Phelps says, "At this time of year, everyone is shopping—the coaches for players and the players for schools. Robey is a fine prospect, but whether we go after him in the spring depends on how we do with Dave Batton in Pennsylvania and Chris Patton in New York. We stand a good chance of getting Rick if we really want him, so now we have to play it cool."

Late in the day, Digger and Terry crowd into a bus with

other Notre Dame personnel for a rainy ride to Tulane Stadium.

* * *

If playing for the national championship is like this, I can hardly wait. I could just feel the excitement and tension. We sat in the middle of the Notre Dame cheering section, and when Alabama went ahead in the second quarter, Don Bouffard, the ticket manager said, "We need a touchdown return by Al Hunter right now." Sure enough, Hunter ran it back all the way, to give Notre Dame the lead at half time.

I spent the third quarter on the sidelines near the Notre Dame bench. It really was impressive to see Ara stay so cool and composed. There was none of that jumping up and down we basketball coaches seem to find necessary. Being so close to the players made me feel like a part of the team, but when Alabama went ahead, I got superstitious and returned to the stands. That's where I was in the fourth quarter when Bob Thomas kicked a nineteen-yard field goal to win it for us, 24–23. After the game, I told Terry to meet me back at the hotel and I hurried to the dressing room. The scene was incredible. Everyone was crying and laughing and yelling all at the same time. It really meant a lot to be inside the dressing room with the national champions. I hope to have that experience with my own players some day.

While snow falls in South Bend, the Phelpses spend the days following the Sugar Bowl on the beaches of Fort Lauderdale. They don't play tennis because the private club where they are staying requires traditional tennis whites—and their sneakers are blue.

The relaxation and anonymity which Digger seeks is easily found. Too easily, in fact. While having cocktails with another couple, the hostess repeatedly calls Notre Dame coach Richard "Digger" Phelps "Trigger."

\* \* \*

It was a wonderful trip. The basketball team beat Kentucky, the football team upset Alabama, and the entire family had a great time in Florida. Rick proved that you can't hunt for seashells in the Atlantic Ocean without getting your thumb wet, but the stitches come out tomorrow.

Terry and I spent most of each day around the pool and on the beach. A few people stopped to talk about the UCLA game and wish us luck, but otherwise it was very relaxing. No basketball, no phone calls, no worries.

The team is in great shape too. How can I complain when we are averaging ninety-two points a game on offense and sixty-eight on defense? The only other Notre Dame team to win seven games and go unbeaten in December played forty years ago.

By now, the players should have complete confidence in their ability to play well and to win. More than anything, I'm pleased with the development of the freshmen. As far as I'm concerned, Dantley is the best one in the country. And he's matured quite a bit too.

Shumate is better than ever; he really knows how to use his power and strength to dominate the boards and the inside game. Still, to play pro ball, he'll have to improve both his one-on-one moves and his dribbling while facing the basket.

Brokaw is doing very well both offensively and defensively. It's amazing that a guard could hit 67 percent of his shots, but Gary is doing it. I'm also pleased with Clay, who continues to make the clutch baskets.

Novak's importance is not revealed in his statistics. We don't expect his averages to be any higher than they are right now—seven points and six rebounds a game. He could score more if we wanted him to, but we have chosen to build the offense around other men. Goose continues to start because he shows great dedication and hustle.

The person I am most concerned about is Crotty, because I know he is unhappy sitting on the bench. Peter would play more if only he asserted himself in the scrimmages between the second and third teams.

Before the season started, I said I would be very pleased if we won twenty games. Since we are already 7–0, I have changed my mind. To win twenty now, we would have to lose six of our last nineteen. This could happen, of course, but I think we'll do better. On the other hand, I do not necessarily want to go unbeaten. If that happened—and it's extremely unlikely—it would create unbearable pressures in the tournament. We lost just one regular season game at Penn in 1970, only to be immediately upset in the tournament by Niagara. I prefer what happened to Florida State two years ago. After playing well all season, the Seminoles lost their last game to Cincinnati and still reached the national finals. I could accept a similar defeat at the end of the year if it relieved the pressure just before the tournament.

## MONDAY, JANUARY 7

Of all the people shoveling snow on Peashway this morning, no one has a better suntan than Digger Phelps.

Later, the first practice of the new year demonstrates the debilitating effect of a long lay-off. The players are slow in their timing; their overall performances are poor.

\* \* \*

I think they returned to school a little too cocky. If not, they must have taken Frank's locker-room posters too seriously. Those scores and comments from opposing coaches are supposed to inspire better play, not swell their heads. I may have to deflate a few egos before we play Xavier on Saturday.

A big problem right now is how to handle the ticket requests for the UCLA game. The ticket manager gives me three hundred for a big game like this; I sell half for him and give half away. Forty-eight of the tickets go to the players: four each to the top seven and senior manager John Palkovics, and two each to the next eight.

## TUESDAY, JANUARY 8

Startling news from the West Coast. Bill Walton injured his back last night during UCLA's 55–45 defeat of Washington State. His status is uncertain for the Bruins' next two games against California and Stanford.

After practice, Phelps tells the team, "I'm sure you have heard about Walton's injury. Well, just remember it's not our concern. We've got two more games before we play UCLA. Let's concentrate on those before we worry about the Bruins."

\* \* \*

I hope Walton will be able to play against us because I can imagine what it would be like if he didn't. If we won, everyone would say it was because he was hurt. If we lost, the Notre Dame fans would say we blew our chance. UCLA is a great team with or without Walton. They proved that against North Carolina State.

### WEDNESDAY, JANUARY 9

This morning, Phelps sits in his office lecturing a physical education class at Anderson College in Anderson, Indiana. By telephone, of course. One of the points he stresses is a coach's need to develop a personal style. "Expose yourself to the books, the clinics, and the camps," he advises, "but in the end, establish your own philosophy. Just be yourself, because you have to believe in yourself to get anything accomplished."

One of the principles Phelps believes in today is that the visiting television reporter from Fort Wayne should not interview his players about UCLA. "We have two more games to play before then," he tells the man. "Come back next week, and you can ask them anything about UCLA you want."

Tonight, while reviewing the Kentucky film, Phelps points out the niggling errors—a foul here, a turnover there, a poor shot somewhere else—that can change the complexion of a game . . . and deflate a few egos.

*   *   *

I received a memo today which upset me. According to Mike Danch, the ACC events manager, we can't practice in the main arena on January 20 and 21. Something about a football rally and a Joni Mitchell concert. Practicing on the auxiliary gym's Tartan floor is no way to prepare for a game on the hard wood floor at Kansas. It may be a small point, but I should have been consulted. I'll take it up with Moose tomorrow.

## THURSDAY, JANUARY 10

The great Athletic and Convocation Center dispute is settled in a meeting among Phelps, Krause, and Joe Sassano, the assistant director of the ACC. They decide that basketball, football, and Joni Mitchell can coexist if Phelps' team practices in the main arena on Sunday night and in the auxiliary gym on Monday morning.

*   *   *

We did not make a point of it to the players, but in today's practice, we began preparing for UCLA. This was possible because Georgetown and UCLA have similar 2-2-1 zone presses. We put Myron Schuckman in Walton's position and told the gold team to attack all the way to the basket. It seemed to work, but then Myron is not Bill Walton. Nor, for that matter, is he Ralph Drollinger, Walton's substitute.

## FRIDAY, JANUARY 11

On his way to the office Phelps, who collects plate block stamps, stops by the post office to pick up a new issue.

Later, he and DiBiaso devise the strategy for Xavier, while McLaughlin is on a recruiting trip to Minnesota. They agree that the Musketeers will probably slow the pace down with controlled play on offense and a zone on defense.

That afternoon, a representative of Gilbert's men's store complains to Phelps because his Saturday television program is cosponsored by its competitor, King's Palace.

\* \* \*

I can't understand what Gilbert's is concerned about. They turned down a chance to sponsor the show before the other store was even asked. Even if King's Palace is the sponsor, I continue to wear and endorse Gilbert's clothes. That is, if they continue to let me.

## SATURDAY, JANUARY 12

Just before sending the team out to play Xavier, Phelps tells the players to dominate from the opening tip-off. "Don't even let them in the game," he orders.

They don't, winning 87–44.

The Irish lead 12–0 after six minutes, 28–8 after thirteen, and 39–20 at the half. Notre Dame is not so much playing well, however, as Xavier is playing poorly. Even so, the Irish roar to a 60–22 advantage with 12:35 left in the game. Less than two minutes later, Phelps brings the carnage to a halt by pulling out the starters.

Novak retires with his best performance of the year. In only nineteen minutes, he scored twelve points, grabbed nine rebounds, blocked seven shots, and helped hold the Musketeers' leading scorer, Mike Plunkett, to two points. In fact, Xavier's entire starting lineup totals only ten.

"We got killed," says Coach Tay Baker. "They just murdered us up and down the court."

\* \* \*

This was one of the best defensive games we've ever played, but our offensive game was very ragged. We can't get away with twenty-four turnovers and poor shot-selection against the better teams.

With Christmas vacation still on, very few students were in the crowd tonight. Most of the ten thousand there must have been townspeople—students are never that quiet. I yelled to Crotty once to "get in the damn game," and I must have been heard all over the arena.

### SUNDAY, JANUARY 13

Phelps puts the team through a vigorous workout for Georgetown, the final test before UCLA. That night, the coaches convene to finalize the Hoya game plan and to begin serious discussion of the Bruins. They spend part of the evening studying film from last year's UCLA games—an 82–56 loss in Los Angeles and an 82–63 defeat in South Bend.

"Walton gets away with whatever he wants," says Phelps wryly.

"But he might not even play Saturday," DiBiaso says. "He missed both their games this weekend."

"And they won anyway," Phelps says. "They are still unbeaten, and they are still UCLA."

\* \* \*

Now comes the most crucial part of our schedule. I wouldn't expect even the NCAA tournament to be this physically and emotionally draining. It isn't enough that we play UCLA twice, as well as Marquette, Kansas, and two other teams who would love to catch us looking ahead, but we have to fly all over the country to do it.

First, we've got to worry about Georgetown. John Thompson's team knocked off St. John's early in the season, and judging by the fact that the Hoyas are already in South Bend, they must be after us too.

Then comes UCLA. To win, we'll need total concentration during each of the following three days. After that game, however, we have only one full day to get ready for Kansas. We'll practice Sunday night the twentieth, fly to Lawrence Monday, play Tuesday, and return Wednesday.

The Jayhawks represent a special problem because they are sandwiched between the two UCLA games. The players will either be down after a loss, wanting another crack at the Bruins, or sky-high after a win, not caring whom they face next.

Having to play St. Francis on the twenty-fourth limits our preparation for the second UCLA game. We fly to

Los Angeles the next day and go at them again the following night.

We'll return from the Coast immediately after the game, arriving early Sunday to begin practice for Marquette that same night. Al McGuire has the Warriors in the Top 10 again, which means still another tough game. I hope we have something left after flying around like a pro team for more than a week.

Some other time, I'll worry about the difficulty of playing four games within seven days after Marquette.

## MONDAY, JANUARY 14

The one person in South Bend certain not to look past Georgetown is Dantley. Adrian knows virtually all the Hoya players from a thousand different playground games. He remembers John Thompson as the coach of the Washington high school power which his own coach refused to play. Some said Morgan Wootten was *afraid* to play St. Anthony's. Now Dantley imagines himself standing alone against Thompson and an opponent with several former St. Anthony's stars.

"All I heard at home over the holidays," says Dantley, "was how they were finally going to get me. I hope we beat them. Maryland beat them by thirty-two points and I want to do it worse."

\* \* \*

Today's was the most unusual practice of my career. While we drilled for Georgetown, Heywood Hale Broun prepared a commentary on Notre Dame basketball for

Digger in the Michigan game with his assistant coaches behind him and Sports Information Director Roger Valdiserri at the table to their left.

The Athletic and Convocation Center at the start of the victory over Marquette.

Seated from left to right: Ray Martin, Bill Paterno, Gary Brokaw, Peter Crotty, John Shumate, Gary Novak, Adrian Dantley, Bill Drew, Dwight Clay, Dave Kuzmicz. Standing from left to right: Student Manager John Palkovics, Assistant Coach Frank McLaughlin, Tom Varga, Greg Schmelzer, Toby Knight, Myron Schuckman, Roger Anderson, Chris Stevens, Ken Wolbeck, Assistant Coach Dick DiBiaso, Head Coach Richard "Digger" Phelps, Trainer Arno Zoske. Missing: Tom Hansen. *(Bagby Photo Company)*

Digger and Terry at the Mideast Region in Tuscaloosa, Alabama.

Digger enjoys a cigar and a laugh with football coach Ara Parseghian.

Digger conducting a practice before the UCLA game in South Bend.

*(Left)* Digger shouts instructions in the miraculous comeback against the Bruins.

*(Below)* Digger reviews strategy in the final minutes before the UCLA game.

*(Bottom)* As Tommy Curtis rushes over to defend, Dwight Clay lofts the corner jump shot which beats UCLA 71-70.
*(Joe Raymond)*

(*Above left*) The players confidently rehearse taking down the net during practice for the Bruins.

(*Above right*) The 71-70 victory complete, Gary Novak is lifted above the crowd to claim a trophy.

(*Below*) The players celebrate in the dressing room after ending UCLA's 88-game winning streak.

*(Above left)* Gary Brokaw.

*(Above)* Gary Novak.

*(Left)* Ray Martin.

*(Top left)* Adrian Dantley.　　*(Top right)* Dwight Clay.

*(Above left)* John Shumate.　　*(Above right)* Bill Paterno.

Digger gets down to business during a time-out in the Kansas triumph.

Digger and Al McGuire each chase a referee in wild win over Marquette.

his CBS broadcast on Saturday evening.

All through practice, his crew shot film, interviewed players, and recorded everything I said on a miniature microphone. It's great to have him out here, but *where* does he get those sports coats?

Speaking of clothes, I went by Gilbert's today and picked out a three-piece plaid suit to wear on Saturday.

## TUESDAY, JANUARY 15

Phelps sits in a South Bend restaurant with UCLA on his mind and three cold meatballs on his plate. For some time, both have gone unattended. "Hey, Digger, how about that football team?" asks yet another intruder. "You gonna win too, aren't ya?" Phelps forces a smile as he looks across the table at DiBiaso.

When the fan leaves, Digger quickly plunges his fork into a meatball with his left hand and opens a blue notebook with his right. But he's caught again. "Hey, Digger, you don't remember me," the next visitor starts, "but I met you two years ago. You looked down then. You're sure looking better now."

At the moment Phelps feels lousy. He is trying very hard to play them one at a time without missing any meals. Finally, the last intruder is gone, the last meatball has surrendered. He and DiBiaso discuss UCLA, whom they have not seen in person since the Bruins established an all-time record with their sixty-first consecutive victory last year.

"I know them so well, I could coach them myself," Phelps says, "and I think I'm learning how to beat them." There is easy agreement about how the Bruins should be played. No slowdowns or stalls. No zones or double-teams. Attack the boards hard on both ends. Don't be afraid to take the play into the middle.

Lunch is about over when DiBiaso makes a suggestion. "We need to do something in practice each day to ease the tension and reward the players for their hard work," he says. "So they can leave with a positive attitude."

Phelps agrees. "Let's try to come up with something special."

The rest of the afternoon is pointed toward Georgetown. "When we upset Marquette last year," Phelps says on the way back to the office, "we were in a situation similar to Georgetown's. We probably caught Al thinking ahead to Minnesota. The win got us going, and that's just what Georgetown wants to happen to them."

At the pregame Mass, Brokaw hangs back as the other players pick up one of the medals which are always blessed before each game.

"Why don't you go up, Gary?" Phelps asks. "Don't you want a medal?"

"No," Brokaw answers. "I haven't taken one all year, and we've won. It might be bad luck to change now."

Phelps spends the last hours before the game at home. "Daddy," says Karen as they sit in the living room, "I don't care about this game tonight. Just beat UCLA so you can be number one."

"But Karen," he answers. "If we lose tonight, beating UCLA might not be enough."

"I don't care. Just beat UCLA."

So ordered, Phelps returns to the ACC, which was dedicated by a thirteen-point loss to UCLA five years ago, and consecrated by a seven-point win over the Bruins two years later. UCLA has not lost a game anywhere since then.

Just before sending the players out on the floor, Phelps says,

"We've worked too hard to get this far and let Georgetown beat us and ruin everything."

The Hoyas have no chance against the clinging Irish press and the powerful inside combination of Shumate and Dantley. The two combine for thirty-three points as Notre Dame bolts to a 61–37 half-time lead. Phelps is afraid to risk injuries just before UCLA, so with 10:20 left, he substitutes for Dantley, Novak, and Clay. Shumate and Brokaw follow two minutes later, and the reserves finish the 104–77 victory.

The final score falls short of the margin Dantley had wanted, even though the Irish lead was thirty-five points and climbing higher when he was taken out. Nevertheless, he can still count the game as a personal triumph because his twenty-two points and ten rebounds surpassed the efforts of every Georgetown player. Due to the Hoyas' unmerciful battering, he registered twelve of his points at the free-throw line.

"Those guys acted like they didn't even care I was out there," says Shumate, who scored twenty-six points. "The only person they tried to stop was Adrian."

Dantley is too tired to say much of anything. "I'm happy, but I'm sore," he says, grimacing as he rubs his shoulder. "It was rough out there."

Phelps' postgame talk is even rougher. The team's win— its ninth straight this season and eleventh in a row at home since the UCLA loss last year—has lifted his Notre Dame record to one modest notch above .500. But he is in no mood to celebrate.

"For the life of me, I can't understand what's wrong with some of you guys," he bellows. "We gave our bench a lot of action tonight, and it was outplayed and outscored. You're not giving a hundred percent. If we call on you and you can't do the job, we'll lose. It's that simple.

"We're playing to win the national championship. It may

take a few knocks and bumps, but if you don't believe in that commitment, then don't interfere with those who do. I think I've been fair to everyone here. Now be fair to me. We're trying to build depth and we're trying to beat UCLA. If you aren't going to give one hundred percent in practice this week, don't even show up.

"Are you *ready* to play UCLA? Don't think about Bill Walton. We're playing U-C-L-A. Are you ready, Shu? Are you ready, Goose? Are you ready, Broke? . . ."

And so on down the line, until every player answers affirmatively. Phelps has not discussed Saturday's game with the players until this moment. As he leaves the room, his face shows a smile unseen by the players. He's psyching them up for The Big Game. The Rock would have loved it.

\* \* \*

Brokaw's reluctance to pick up a medal after Mass reminds me of my own superstition about red cardinals. If I see one just before a game, I'm more confident about winning. I guess that's why I have a bird-feeder in my back yard and a cardinal figurine in my office. Robins and sparrows are nice, but give me a bright red cardinal any day.

## WEDNESDAY, JANUARY 16

Notre Dame students starting the new semester are greeted all over town by marquees which proclaim the football team's Sugar Bowl victory. That game and others set for this weekend remind many seniors of the spectacular athletic upsets which occurred in their freshman year. The football team defeated top-ranked Texas in the Cotton Bowl. The hockey team shocked number-one Denver. And the basketball team ended UCLA's nineteen-game winning streak.

Now, three years later, history may soon repeat itself. The football team has already defeated top-ranked Alabama. Friday night, the hockey team faces number-one Michigan Tech. And UCLA is due in soon with an eighty-eight-game winning streak.

While McLaughlin returns from scouting Kansas, Phelps and DiBiaso evaluate last night's game. They note that the backcourt made too many turnovers (twelve), that there was not enough penetration on offense, and that the team did not get back quickly enough on defense. When Brokaw is mentioned, Phelps says, "Sometimes Gary doesn't concentrate on what he's doing. When he does, he is really something."

Next, they discuss the UCLA game-plan. Notre Dame hopes to force UCLA to the left, away from Keith Wilkes and toward Walton's low-post position. Shumate will set up behind Walton, overplaying him to the right to keep him off the baseline. When Walton moves to the left with his back to the basket, Shumate must force him out as far as he can.

"Our objective is to take away the lob pass and not worry if Walton gets twenty-five points," says Phelps. "I'm more concerned about Wilkes, anyway. Shumate can't let this become a crusade, him against Walton. If Walton beats us with ten hook shots, let him." They do not consider that Walton might not play. "That's the media's problem, not mine," says Phelps.

Wilkes will be Novak's problem. Dantley will check the taller Meyers, while Clay and Brokaw pick up Curtis and Trgovich. "In my humble opinion," Phelps says, repeating his private sentiment, "UCLA just is not as good as it has been."

Phelps and DiBiaso move to the blackboard in Dick's office, and translate their ideas into *X*s and *O*s. The cramped quarters become an imaginary court where they portray the defensive position Shumate is to take against Walton.

The mood changes after lunch when Phelps talks on the phone to Crotty. "Peter, I just want you to know I do care about what you're going through," he begins. "You're like a brother to me, and I'm dying to see you score more. It's a crisis for you, sure, but bear with it. Don't lose your confidence. It's not that big a deal, really.

"I haven't lost faith in you. Everything is time and patience. The right time and the right place will come. Just wait. I really respect what you've done for us here. We want to be successful, and what you're doing is important to that goal."

When the players arrive for practice, each finds a three-by-five card taped to his locker. Novak's reads "Stop Wilkes." Brokaw's, "Good Shots." Clay's, "No Turnovers." Dantley's, "Boards." Shumate's, "Defense-Boards."

"Digger has given us confidence by saying we are going to play UCLA straight up," Shumate says as he pulls on his support stocking. "I thought some of the things we did last year played right into their hands." Standing nearby, Dantley admits he's glad he didn't have to face UCLA earlier. "If I had gone to Maryland and played them in my first college game, I wouldn't have been ready. Now I am. I've thought about them a lot since we beat Indiana."

One practice drill gives the gold team ball-possession with three minutes to go and an eight-point lead. The blue team presses, but the regulars hold on to win. "You know what happens now?" Phelps asks. "Shu, you go to one basket, and Goose, you go to the other. The rest of you lift them up like they're cutting down the net." As the players enact the gimmick DiBiaso was looking for, Phelps says, "Don't let me down. That's where I want you after the game Saturday."

Practice concludes with a free-spirited game of "Irish

basketball" in which opposing teams try to pass the ball to a player in the middle of the foul circle without ever dribbling. As Greg Schmelzer, a perennial blue-teamer, changes into an unfamiliar gold shirt, he says, "If I'm not careful, this will give me an identity crisis."

One more chore remains. After dinner the team views the. first ten minutes of last year's games with UCLA. In the whirring darkness, the Bruins take the lead both times, but the advantages are slight. The slaughters are performed on later reels, unseen, as if they never happened. Phelps points out the referees' calls which cost Notre Dame points, effective play which won them, and the precision with which the Irish pierced the UCLA press. He tells them not to worry about the lob to Walton, that "it has been taken right out of their game." He says Wilkes is not nearly so effective when pressured, that he does not like to play one-on-one.

The players' imaginations stir in response to this litany of Bruin deficiencies. Paterno imagines himself driving on Walton. Martin winds through the Bruin press. "You've got to believe you can beat them after watching this film," Phelps says. The lights come on and the players clap. As they walk out Brokaw says, "I can't wait."

\* \* \*

DiBiaso made a comment tonight which described my own feelings. "I feel like it's Friday," he told me. "I think we're prepared. I'm ready." I think we all are.

## THURSDAY, JANUARY 17

Phelps and his staff want to be prepared for anything. "If we were ahead late in the game and in our delay offense," Digger asks in the morning meeting, "how would UCLA react? Would Walton follow Shumate up high or would he stay low to stop the drives and get the rebounds?" The coaches decide Walton would stay low.

McLaughlin, back from his scouting trip, says little until it's time to report on Kansas' 73–69 win over Iowa State. There is a strange irony when Phelps, whose attitude about UCLA has been so positive, so confident, asks "Can we beat Kansas, Frank?"

"We can, Digger," he answers, "but it will be tough to do on their court."

McLaughlin says that the Jayhawks' best asset is their big men, but that "they aren't as good as ours. Our pressure defense should force a lot of turnovers, but the game will be decided on the boards. We'll have to box out. They try to confuse teams by changing defenses a lot, but they tend to foul. We should work on our free-throw shooting in practice. Offensively, they have good open shooters like Indiana's. Rick Suttle, their leading scorer last year, isn't even starting now, but [Ted] Owens brings him off the bench."

After McLaughlin finishes his report a few minutes later, the meeting ends and the distractions begin. One quarter of Phelps' work day is given to the press, whose most-frequent question is, "Do you think Walton will play?" Phelps patiently explains that he doesn't care. Other people call about tickets. He says he has none left. "The ticket manager tells me we could sell fifty thousand if we had them," Phelps comments. One of the ticket inquiries is from a lady who claims to be Pete Trgovich's mother. "I've lost mine," she says to Dottie. "Could Coach Phelps help?" Digger declines the call, saying, "Take it up with the ticket manager."

The hassle is even worse for the players, who have no secretaries to screen calls and no assistants to eliminate minor irritations. "It's getting ridiculous," Shumate says. "One guy said he was Bill Walton." Clay is trying hard to be cool during the commotion, but he admits, "The students are getting me too excited." Dwight would like to play down the significance of the game. "Even if we do win, we won't deserve any special attention. There's still a long way to go before the season's over."

When Clay makes a bad pass in practice this afternoon, Phelps is all over him. As they stand at midcourt Dwight says quietly, "Don't worry, Coach. I'll be ready."

"All right," Phelps answers, "get back in and do the job."

Digger is trying to keep the players alert. He explodes again when the first team loses its lead in the last-minute delay drill the coaches had discussed that morning. Digger stops practice in a rage. "I'll be damned if I'll lose a lead like this. If you don't want to play UCLA, let me know and I'll get you St. Mary's. I'll give you every pressure situation you'll face, and you better be ready to react."

One of those situations is called "spurt time," a burst of hustle in which a team tries to build a quick lead or recover from a large deficit. Press, steal, score; then set up and do it again. The drill works well.

After practice, the coaches drive to Chicago to see UCLA against Iowa. "I'll have to disguise myself when we get there," Phelps jokes on the way. "Should I sell hot dogs, or walk in with a fat lady?" Once there, he does neither, choosing instead to sit in the empty bleachers well behind one of the baskets.

When the first game of the doubleheader between Oral Roberts and Loyola ends, Loyola assistant coach Buzzy O'Connor walks laboriously toward his team's dressing room, passing finally underneath the stands where Phelps sits. Digger knows O'Connor, and is aware of his terminal illness. After the three coaches return from greeting him, Phelps shakes his head and says, "That is so sad." Until three years ago, O'Connor was Johnny Dee's assistant. After Dee left, O'Connor had to quit so Phelps could form his own staff. [The Loyola assistant died a few months later.]

UCLA defeats Iowa, 68–44, but Walton—who has made the trip East—does not come to the game. "I really don't care if he plays or not," Phelps says after making an early exit for South Bend, "but I think he's going to. I don't know what all this secret stuff has been about, but I think he's going to play."

Back in his dorm, Myron Schuckman is also thinking about Walton. While lying on his bed, he pictures every move he knows the great center can make. People are saying that Myron has never been better since he assumed Walton's role in practice.

\* \* \*

When I walked in the door late tonight, I found Terry downstairs asleep on the couch. After she woke up, we just sat there a while, not saying much, just looking at each other. She understands how I feel and what this game means. It was just nice, that's all.

## FRIDAY, JANUARY 18

Phelps stops by the Golden Dome on his way to work, not to pay homage but to greet the administrators and secretaries in the development office. "Are you girls going to be there tomorrow?" he calls to a room of typists.

"Wish we could, Digger," one of them answers, "but we have to work."

"Then pray," he says. "You can always pray."

At the office, Phelps opens a telegram from the Notre Dame Club of Los Angeles, an embattled minority in Bruin territory. "We in Los Angeles wish you and your team continued success," he reads. "We are proud of your accomplishments."

There is nothing new to discuss in the coaches' meeting. "The kids are ready," Digger says. "We can stay with what we have done."

Phelps is loose and confident at a noon press luncheon. "After we went 6–20, I thought about going to embalming school," he jokes. Asked about the kind of officiating he would like to have, he cracks, "Two homers." Of the game against UCLA next week, he observes, "Considering the energy crisis, it's our national duty not to show up."

Phelps is more serious when asked the inevitable question about Walton's status. "Ten years from now, no one will remember who played," he answers, "but they will remember that Notre Dame won."

Today's practice is not as sharp as yesterday's. Phelps abruptly ends a scrimmage in which the blue team is pressing the golds hard. Nevertheless, the net-cutting scenario is repeated, reminding Digger of a picture in his office which shows Austin Carr taking down the cord trophy after the UCLA game three years ago. At that moment, the court was a sea of pushing, shoving, cheering, delirious students. Among them was Shumate, who had rushed down from the stands to help lift Carr up. Phelps has often wondered what it was like to see such great emotion unleashed.

He gets an indication a few hours later when three thousand students pour into bare, round Stepan Center for a pep rally. The crowd presses against the island platform where the players, coaches, and guests sit. Among them are Phelps' mother and father and Sid Catlett, who has not seen a home game since he left school three years ago. After the band marches in to the rousing cadence of the Irish fight song, after twelve cheerleaders and one costumed leprechaun have warmed the audience with their appeals to school pride,

Catlett rises to speak. "I have a telegram," he tells the churning students below him. "It says, 'Sorry, John, I won't be able to play with you tomorrow. I've got a yellow streak coming on. Signed, Bill Walton.'" The crowd roars.

Shumate is next. "Clay wanted me to tell you something," he announces. Then, jumping up and clicking his heels, Shu says, "We're going to help UCLA 'kick the habit.'"

Novak steps forward to predict that "after Saturday's game, Walton is going to have one helluva traumatic experience." Goose adds, "People say UCLA has defense, strength, and quickness. Well, that was said about another team—Alabama."

It is left to Chris Stevens—the closest thing the team has to a free spirit—to put the game into perspective. Clad in overalls, Hawk walks to the microphone and says boldly, "This game is so important, Fr. Hesburgh is making a guest appearance on campus."

That really sets everyone off.

Finally, it is Phelps' turn. After a minute of cheering, he pledges that since "you never let us down, believe me, we won't let you down."

The Alma Mater is played, the band wakes up the echoes for the eleventh time, and the pep rally is over. When Phelps steps down from the stage, he is met by three students, who will "do anything" to get into the game. Phelps, who has had "no more" tickets all week, reaches into his pocket and produces three.

The players return to their dorm rooms. The first floor of Fisher Hall is calmer than usual this Friday night. Shumate personally quiets five parties and appoints monitors to keep peace so he can sleep. Two floors up, Clay and Brokaw consider going to a movie, then decide to stay in.

For several thousand others, there is just enough time after the rally to get to the hockey game against Michigan Tech. Notre Dame wins 7–1.

* * *

Nineteen days ago I was wondering how Ara felt just before the Alabama game. Now I know: on edge, a little nervous, and very anxious to play.

The night before last year's game, Wooden and I taped a Gilbert's commercial together. I thought we would do it again this year, but I was never called.

I met Wooden while working at a basketball camp in the Pennsylvania Poconos the summer before I went to Penn. He had come there to lecture, and I was anxious to meet him and see what he was like. As he talked, it became clear that his coaching technique emphasizes fundamentals and constant practice drills.

It was Vince Lombardi's philosophy all over again: a team will win if it executes better than its opponent.

I never considered that I might coach against him some day. He had already won two national championships, and I was two years out of college.

Now, it's seven and a half years later and he's won every NCAA title since. But while he's stayed the same, so to speak, I've joined the chase after him. In a way, my entire college coaching career has been pointed toward beating him. Wooden has been the man on top every year I've been in the profession.

I have tremendous respect for what he has accomplished, as a player and as a coach. Living in Indiana, where so many people remember and admire him, it is impossible not to. Wooden's records will never be equaled.

Nevertheless, I disagree with many of the things he does. Everyone realizes Wooden has mastered the game; he acts as if he invented it as well. He's so sanctimonious, a priest told me before the Georgetown game, "We play the Jesuits on Tuesday and God on Saturday."

While Wooden sits on the bench clutching that silver cross in his hand, he's also riding officials and players worse than any other coach I have seen. I warned Shumate today not to walk past the UCLA bench during time-outs, because I don't want Wooden taking verbal shots at him. That's so bush-league for a man of his stature, yet no referee has the nerve to reprimand him.

Many people saw this other side of Wooden on television last year, when he walked down to our bench during the game and threatened to send Swen Nater after Shumate. He must have realized how uncalled-for that was, because he later wrote me an apology.

I wonder what Wooden's reaction will be if we upset them tomorrow. He knows so little about losing, he thinks he has to make an excuse every time it happens. After Houston beat his team in 1968, he said it was because "Lewis" Alcindor (Kareem Abdul-Jabbar) was injured. When it happened here in 1971, it was because their bus got lost between Chicago and South Bend. I'm sure if we do it tomorrow, it will be because Walton was injured—no matter how well he plays.

### SATURDAY, JANUARY 19

At 6:30 A.M., Shumate is roused by a ringing telephone. His parents are calling from Elizabeth, N.J., and for fifteen minutes they talk about the game. In the small, dark room John is told that no matter what happens today, he should maintain confidence and faith in himself, that he can lose a game but not his pride. When he hangs up, Shumate is wide awake. He turns his tape deck to full volume, opens the door, and yells out, "Wake up, everybody. It's Bruin time!"

The pregame Mass is said by Fr. Joyce in the crypt chapel of Sacred Heart Church. "This is not an ordinary day," he tells the team. "Chances are, you will look back on this day as one of the memorable ones in your life." Fr. Joyce prays for "the grace to do our best, to contribute to the success of the team" and not for personal help. Novak, who had given Walton hell at last night's pep rally, this morning gives his team a reading from Hebrews.

Two hours later, Goose enters the locker room singing, "Oh, Happy Day." The air is heavy with the smell of Tru-Balm, a heating salve. Shumate tells a manager to turn up the tape deck. "I need music to psyche me up." Brokaw joins John in singing a familiar lyric. Stevens is juking to the rhythm. Clay slowly puts on his uniform, nodding with the beat. The freshmen dress quietly, slightly bewildered.

Suddenly, Shumate yells out, "I had a dream last night, brothers."

The players immediately assume the role of Pentecostal worshipers. "Tell it, brother!"

"I dreamed I was running from a big bear."

"Yeah!"

"He had me scared for a while."

"We know. We know."

"I ran into the woods, and there was a leprechaun there."

"Tell it, brother."

"I said, 'Lep, a bear is after me. What can I do?' "

"Yeah!"

"The lep said, 'Shu, lay down a Bear Bryant trap.' "

"Tell it!"

"So I lay down a Bear Bryant trap and the trap say, 'Snap!' "

What the parable lacks in religiosity, it surpasses in symbolic fervor. Meanwhile, Phelps is hurriedly writing the team's game plan on the blackboard. He lists six things the players must do to win. He reminds them of four that will cost them the game—the first and most important is a warning against losing poise and confidence. About eleven o'clock, Digger says, "All right, let's go to work." The music is turned off and in calm, reassuring tones he reviews the orders of the day.

The players clap as they leave to loosen up. The first sight of the team brings a cheer from the fans filling the arena. Among them is Fr. James Burtchaell, the university provost, who is here to see his first Notre Dame game ever. On the nearby St. Mary's campus, eight nuns are gathering to watch the game on television and, as they have all year, they pray very hard.

When the team returns for its final instructions, Phelps warns them to stay away from the UCLA bench.

"All right," he says. "I want you to act like men, play like men, and win like men." It is 11:56 when the men storm onto the court.

Fittingly, this confrontation between the only unbeaten teams in the Top 20 is taking place on "College Basketball Day." A capacity crowd of 11,343 and a TVS audience of 13.5 million will see two paragons of a sport reputedly played for the first time on January 19, 1892, in Springfield, Mass. UCLA is 13–0, Notre Dame 9–0, and each has an average winning margin of twenty-six points.

The team's differences are reflected in their coaches, who stand at midcourt, separated by two television interviewers. One a brash young warrior in light plaid, the other dark-suited, the venerable chief. Before the interviews begin, Wooden repeatedly leans out to catch Phelps' eye. Digger seems not to notice. He measures the crowd, studies his team, refuses to acknowledge the gesture.

As the squads take their last warm-up shots before the

player introductions, two Notre Dame students circle the court with a bedsheet sign that reads:

Dear John Wooden,
God DID make Notre Dame #1.
Sincerely,
Paul "Bear" Bryant

The Bruins hardly notice. Their cool, professional approach is personified by Walton, who is whistling confidently along with the Irish pep band. Even with his upper back braced, the redhead sees no reason why today's game should be any different from the previous 139 he has played since his junior year in high school.

Sixteen seconds after the tip-off, Dave Meyers puts UCLA ahead with a jump shot from the top of the key. Notre Dame is quick to challenge Walton underneath, and during a wild scramble, the Bruin center catches an elbow in the face as Dantley's lay-up ties the score. The game stops while Walton's bleeding lip is mended.

The Irish stay even through the first four minutes, but six and a half minutes later they are behind 25–14 and Phelps must call time-out. UCLA has built its lead on baskets by the two players who concerned Digger the least: Trgovich and Meyers. Trgovich sneaked backdoor twice on Brokaw, and Meyers hit all five shots he tried against Dantley. Further, Curtis has proven that the lob pass to Walton is still very much in the Bruin repertoire. Wilkes, meanwhile, is already three baskets to the good against Novak.

After play resumes, Notre Dame's condition becomes even worse. UCLA extends its lead to seventeen points, 33–16, and with 6:41 remaining, Digger's team seems headed toward an early burial. During the next six minutes, however, the Irish revive and outscore the Bruins 18–6. While Notre Dame sizzles, UCLA's baskets come only from Walton—on another lob and follow-ups of missed shots by Trgovich and Wilkes.

Martin hits from twenty feet, Brokaw converts a fast-break pass, Clay banks in a missed free-throw, Shumate powers over Walton, and Paterno bombs from twenty-five. The assault also includes four foul shots by Dantley, Clay, and Brokaw, and a pair of basket-interference and goal-tending violations by the ever-present Walton.

Notre Dame's aggressive play becomes costly after the score reaches 39–34. Fouls by Paterno and Martin in the last thirty-four seconds lead to four free throws by Wilkes and Greg Lee, giving UCLA a nine-point half-time advantage.

The Bruins seem more vulnerable than the 43–34 score might indicate. They built their margin by hitting nineteen of twenty-seven shots, an incredible 70 percent rate not likely to continue. And the Irish awakening late in the period demonstrated their true ability.

Phelps has all of this in mind when he talks to the team during intermission. As the players devour oranges and Hershey bars, Digger tells them, "You should have all the confidence in the world you can win. I want the same intensity, the same desire and the same game plan."

Encouragement is just what Shumate needs. It has been a difficult twenty minutes for Shu, who made only four of eleven shots and was outscored and out-rebounded by Walton 12–8 and 6–4. Clay comes over to tell him, "Stick with it, Big Daddy. You can do it."

Shumate says nothing.

Phelps decides to start Martin in place of Novak in the second half, and to put Brokaw on Wilkes. Novak did not contribute a point or a rebound in the first half, while Wilkes was scoring ten and helping Walton on the boards with three. Phelps realizes the change will only aggravate the height disadvantage, but he wants Martin's speed and defensive quickness in the game.

On the arena floor, meanwhile, Ara Parseghian is accepting the Grantland Rice Trophy from Tom McEwen, president of the Football Writers Association of America. At first sight of Parseghian, the Notre Dame students begin cheering: "Ara, change the score! Ara, change the score! Ara, change the score!"

Ara, who once coached freshman basketball at Miami of Ohio, is unable to.


Phelps' lineup adjustments pay off immediately, as the Irish open the second half by outscoring the Bruins 9–2. Six points are Brokaw's (two following a steal by Martin) and he almost ties the game at 45-all when a jump shot rims in and out.

UCLA regains control after the miss, shutting out Notre Dame the next four and a half minutes and taking an eleven-point lead. Walton, dominant as ever, scores three of the baskets.

Shumate finally ends the Irish drought with an eighteen-foot jumper at 10:44 and, with Brokaw, sparks still another Irish comeback. The margin is down to six with 5:24 left, when Notre Dame's hopes suffer a severe jolt. After commiting his fourth foul, Brokaw raises both arms, an automatic technical that sends Wilkes to the line with an extra free-throw opportunity. Wilkes makes only two of his three shots, however, and the Irish are spared further distress when the Bruins blow their bonus chance from the field. A minute later, Shumate draws a foul while beating Walton inside for the fourth time in the half. He completes the three-point play, and the Irish are within five, 64–59.

UCLA responds with six straight points, four by Curtis, whose corner jumper with 3:32 left gives the Bruins a 70–59 lead. That basket—his first of the half—does more to hurt the Irish than any of the bad-mouthing and finger-pointing he has dished out all afternoon.

Phelps calls time ten seconds later and tells Martin to

report back in for Paterno, who had replaced him earlier. The change will give Notre Dame the same quick, pressing lineup that was so effective at the end of the first half and start of the second. Phelps kneels down in front of the team and orders fullcourt pressure with Shumate guarding Walton on inbound plays. "Don't give up," he yells over the din of the crowd. "Spurt time can win it. We're gonna win. We're gonna win."

At 3:07 Shumate gets the ball inside, wheels, and scores on Walton. It is 70–61.

At 2:57 Shumate steals the inbounds pass and scores his twenty-fourth point, equaling Walton's output. It is 70–63.

At 2:22 Dantley intercepts a pass intended for Wilkes, dribbles three quarters of the court, and scores. It is 70–65.

At 2:16 Curtis gets behind the Irish press, catches a long pass, and scores easily—but the points are nullified by a walking violation. It is still 70–65.

At 2:01 Brokaw shoots over Wilkes from the left corner and scores. It is 70–67.

At 1:25 Meyers shoots and misses, and Shumate rebounds. It is still 70–67.

At 1:11 Brokaw dribbles to the middle, stops at the free-throw line, shoots, and scores his twenty-fifth point. It is 70–69.

At 0:45 Wilkes drives and appears to make his third basket of the half—but the points are nullified because he charged into Martin. It is still 70–69.

At 0:30 Brokaw, unable to get the ball inside to Shumate, passes to Clay, who is open deep in the right corner and anxious to shoot. At 0:29 the Iceman releases a soft, arching shot, before Curtis, racing over, can slam into him and knock him off the court. Unlike his first field-goal attempt of the game, which missed the basket entirely, this one drops through the net—just as it had against Marquette, Pittsburgh and Ohio State. It is 71–70, and there is bedlam all around.

Dwight scrambles back up, realizing that plenty of time remains for UCLA to regain the lead.

After the basket—and three minutes after Notre Dame's miraculous comeback began—Wooden finally calls time-out. At the Irish bench, DiBiaso suggests fouling Walton to test his ability to make both ends of a one-and-one. After all, Walton has made only 43 percent of his attempts this year.

Phelps declines the risk, and reminds the team to immediately call time-out if UCLA scores.

When play resumes, Shumate almost intercepts the inbound pass again, but Curtis comes up with it and hurriedly fires a long outside shot which misses. Meyers follows and misses, and the ball goes out of bounds . . . off Brokaw.

UCLA brings the ball in to Walton, who attempts an awkward turnaround shot, eight feet out and at a slight right angle to the basket. He misses for only the second time in the game. Trgovich taps and misses. Meyers follows and misses. When Shumate cradles his eleventh rebound, the game is over.

As the wild Irish rogues pour onto the floor, it is 1971 all over again. Phelps jumps onto DiBiaso. McLaughlin hurries to the dressing room. Brokaw is in the arms of his father; Clay, his mother. At one end of the court Novak, who did not play at all in the second half, is taking down the net, just as he had practiced all week. But Shumate is not to be found. Pounded in the crush, he is fighting his way to the dressing room to ask for smelling salts. It is Dantley who is lofted to the net at the other end.

After beating Indiana, the Notre Dame players were merely jubilant; now they indulge in a body-hugging, palm-slapping, laughing, shouting frenzy similar to the delirious scene Phelps enjoyed after the Sugar Bowl. In fact, standing in the middle of the celebration is Eric Penick, the football team's star halfback. Off to the side, Sid Catlett shakes his head back and forth saying, "I can't believe it. It's just like three years ago."

Phelps steps in and asks for quiet; his praise tumbles out all at once. "It was the intensity, men, the intensity. You never quit. You never lost your poise. I don't care what you do tonight, just let me get a good night's sleep. I don't want a call at three or four o'clock in the morning telling me you're in jail."

The players can barely comprehend their accomplishment. "I can't believe it," says Brokaw. "This is like nothing I have ever experienced," says Novak. "It feels great, unbelievable," says Clay. "This is the greatest feeling I have ever had in my life," says Shumate.

The emotions of the UCLA players are hidden by Wooden's closed-door dressing-room policy. When they finally emerge, their comments are strained. "They played a good game and they won," Wilkes says softly. "That's all we can say." Curtis adds, "The streak had to end sometime."

The coaches give their comments in a makeshift interview-room which is normally a women's dressing lounge. Pressed on to a counter by an anxious mob of reporters and cameramen, Phelps rejoices, "It was a great win for eighty-eight other coaches, and it was great for college basketball. I'm sure a lot of people around the country were rooting for us today. It's only human nature to want to see the Bruins beaten. Everybody wanted to see the Yankees lose once in a while."

Phelps is still talking and sweating when Wooden arrives for his interview. Because they did not see each other in the crush after the game, Phelps goes over to greet him.

"You don't mind if we don't show up next week, do you?" Digger grins.

"You'd better," says Wooden with a wry smile.

The UCLA coach is much less ruffled than Phelps, and his professorial demeanor remains intact.

"If I said it once, I said it a hundred times," he begins.

"Once we broke the record last year, the streak was meaningless."

He points out the two "tough calls" which erased baskets that would have "salted it away." UCLA, he says, did not lose its poise late in the game, nor was it bothered by the Irish crowd. He didn't call for a time-out because "I am not a time-out fellow."

He admits he did not expect to lose after leading by eleven points with over three minutes left. "We lost a little of our drive and played a little too conservatively. . . . We just stopped playing well. . . . We beat ourselves to some degree." Notre Dame came on when "Brokaw got hot and they started getting the ball in to Shumate better."

Wooden complains that his other players did not have sufficient opportunity to practice with Walton, that his center (who hit twelve of fourteen shots and had nine rebounds in a full forty-minute performance) "wasn't up to par" and "lacked his usual mobility." He concludes ominously, "We'll know a little more about the two teams Saturday, when maybe he's feeling better."

Wooden says he will vote Notre Dame number one in the UPI coaches' poll, but that the Irish are not better than Maryland. He reminds everyone that Notre Dame "had to struggle to win at home" and predicts, "If we win at home, it will prove we will have a better chance on a neutral court."

Wooden disagrees that ending the Bruin streak—even though it had become "meaningless"—was good for basketball. "It was one of the greatest things" the college game ever had. Without it, "there wouldn't have been this much interest and excitement today."

Finally, he says he is a little surprised by the way the streak ended. "I didn't think we would lose outside the conference."

In sum, it is vintage Wooden.

After the game, approximately 450 people show up at the Phelps' open house—among them the governor of Indiana,

Dr. Otis Bowen. Phelps spends half his time on the telephone with such well-wishers as Parseghian, and the other half greeting the parade of people marching through the door. He stops only long enough to watch Heywood Hale Broun's report on the evening news, updated at the last minute to include the Irish victory.

On campus, two players who did not even get into the game, Bill Drew and Toby Knight, receive a standing ovation when they enter the South Dining Hall for dinner. Clay and Brokaw party in one of the dormitories. Shumate goes on a date. And Novak and Crotty celebrate with half a bottle of Southern Comfort—agreeing to save the rest until after Notre Dame wins the national championship.

\* \* \*

We won. I was confident before the game, and I never gave up hope when we fell behind, but it's still a little hard to believe. Maybe I was just too dumb to recognize a hopeless situation.

Right now, I'm tired—physically and mentally worn out. And I'm happier than I've been after any other game I ever watched, played, or coached.

But frankly, it's impossible to completely appreciate what's happened. I keep thinking about the Kansas game on Tuesday and, of course, UCLA again next Saturday.

I could enjoy this one more if it had been played in Greensboro on March 25. Still, we won, and that's all that matters right now. We got some breaks, of course, but a team always does when it wins a close game. The important thing is that the kids never lost their poise. I've always felt that UCLA could be beaten if their opponents refused to give up easily.

This game definitely proves we've got a shot at the national championship.

## SUNDAY, JANUARY 20

Ara Parseghian's second national championship football team is honored in an afternoon rally at the ACC. Assorted high school title-winners from across Indiana are recognized, too, by such dignitaries as Governor Bowen and the mayors of South Bend, Mishawaka, and Elkhart.

Digger, who had earlier declined an invitation to sit on the podium, is now a last-minute honoree. He is greeted by a huge cheer when introduced to the crowd. Fittingly, two gold-on-blue banners hang overhead, proclaiming, "IRISH #1."

The coaches' meeting before the evening practice is subdued. There is almost no indication that Notre Dame has done anything more than win just another game. The offense, it is decided, was not hurt by the UCLA press. The Irish press, especially with Martin in the game, is judged very effective. Wilkes was much less a problem after Brokaw took over for Novak. (In the second half, Wilkes shot two-for-nine, while Brokaw was six-for-eight. Both grabbed two rebounds, and Wilkes had one more turnover.)

The analysis continues with the observation that Shumate played Walton to a standoff, fronting him sometimes and playing behind him at others. Meyers is more physical than expected. Trgovich is the least of their worries. Generally, the Irish could have played better.

And, like that, UCLA is forgotten. The coaches move to McLaughlin's office to watch the film at last year's Kansas game. In the flickering light, it is hard to imagine that the team struggling to beat Kansas in overtime for only its second victory in eight games, could be the same one which defeated UCLA yesterday. But there they are—Shumate, Brokaw, Clay, and Novak—younger, less capable, unaware of the ability that lies within them.

It is a proud and confident team that takes the practice

floor a half hour later. It is also a tired one, drained by Saturday night's celebration. "I got in at five," says Shumate wearily, "and the phone was still ringing." The only mention of the team's new place in the college basketball universe is made by Phelps. He predicts a funeral Tuesday if the team does not shape up. "I'll be damned if we're going to lose to Kansas," he shouts. Easing off a bit during wind sprints, Phelps admits that yes, Notre Dame is working hard, showing the virtues of a number-one team.

At ten o'clock, practice ends. The players grin as they move to centercourt for the traditional cheer. "All right," says Phelps, smiling self-consciously. "The first time ever. . . . Number one?"

"Notre Dame!"

"Number one?"

"Notre Dame!"

"Number one?"

"Notre Dame!"

\* \* \*

I have finally thought of something good about the Kansas trip tomorrow. I won't be in the office to hear the phone ring. It's going to be a madhouse for Dottie.

## MONDAY, JANUARY 21

The trip from South Bend to Lawrence, Phelps once said, is the "worst in basketball." Today, it is even more so, because the team's Chicago–to–Kansas City flight has been canceled. After six hours spent waiting, riding in buses, and flying in airplanes, Notre Dame arrives weary and hungry.

Among the pile of messages awaiting Phelps at the motel is one very welcome bit of news: for the first time in three years, a new team sits atop the Associated Press poll. Notre Dame drew thirty-six first-place votes for 990 points, while UCLA received fifteen for 944.

Practice on the raised floor of Allen Field House, however, fails to reveal the stuff of which national champions are made. The players are listless, motivated not at all by the Jayhawks' six straight wins, 11–3 record, and Big Eight leadership. Phelps is angry. "There are going to be seventeen thousand people wanting to see you beaten tomorrow," he shouts. "You'd better be ready." Afterwards, he is more soothing. "Way to go, John. . . . Atta boy, Broke. . . . Way to hit the boards, Adrian."

More than anything, Phelps wants to march into Los Angeles the way UCLA came to South Bend, unbeaten and unmistakably number one.

* * *

Before we left today, Moose Krause came down to my office to wish us luck. "Keep her going," he said, "and have a nice trip." Well, the trip was lousy, and I'm not sure we can keep her going.

## TUESDAY, JANUARY 22

An hour's shooting practice on the morning of a road game loosens up a team and familiarizes it with new surroundings. There are no drills, no scrimmages, no discussions of strategy.

The coaches have nothing to do but tell the players when to shoot at the other basket.

This morning's session—attended by two admiring Kansas cheerleaders—is proceeding just as routinely when a reporter comments to McLaughlin about yesterday's poor workout. Phelps, who is sitting beside them at the scorer's table, interrupts sharply. "What does yesterday's practice have to do with the game today?" he says to the writer. "That's forgotten, over with. Who cares about that?"

The reporter stands up and walks away. Later, as the players prepare to return to the motel, McLaughlin offers some advice. "Digger didn't mean anything by it," he tells the reporter. "That's just how he is sometimes. When he gets like this, Dick and I just stay out of his way."

In the dressing room before the game, Phelps seems as frenzied as he was calm on Saturday. "Everything will be going against you," he warns the team. "They have the crowd, and they have the emotion. Just think how bad you would feel if you lost to them. You'd be dying for an opportunity to play them again. You'd want to beat them more than anyone in the country. So don't make the mistake of losing to them tonight."

As the players leave, Brokaw urges his teammates, "All right, let's show these guys what it's like to be number one."

For twenty devastating minutes they do, playing almost perfect basketball to establish a 49–35 lead. Notre Dame makes 59 percent of its shots from the floor and all fifteen attempts from the foul line, while harassing Kansas into 36 percent shooting and ten turnovers. At half time, Phelps tells the team not to let up, but when play resumes, their earlier intensity is gone.

Rick Suttle, who had come off the bench to score Kansas' last six points in the first half, continues to dominate Shumate. His five baskets help the Jayhawks close to 61–59 with 10:35

remaining. Seconds later, Shumate leaves the game with his fourth foul, and the crowd of 17,100 roars expectantly.

But while John languishes on the bench, the Irish refuse to fold. When he returns almost six minutes later, their lead has actually been extended to four points, 71–67. At McLaughlin's suggestion, Phelps orders the four-corner delay offense, and Notre Dame holds on to win 76–74.

After the game, Phelps' relief is obvious. "It's a super win," he praises the team. "I don't care if it was by one or thirty." Then he warns them not to give the press "anything UCLA can use for its locker-room bulletin board."

"If we were on any kind of cloud," says Martin, "we're sure enough down to earth now." In another corner of the room, Dantley frets about the two one-and-one free throws he missed near the end of the game.

"That crowd is a monster, man," Clay, the veteran, tells him. "It's gotta be just you and the rim."

Shumate is only too happy to see the game end. He collected a meager three rebounds as the Irish were dominated on the boards 42–23, and he did little to contain Suttle, who boosted his seven-point scoring average with twenty-seven points. "I got my head handed to me tonight," he says glumly. "I'm just glad the team didn't lose because of my bad play. I'm humbled, man, to the level where I should have been before."

Back at the motel, Phelps finally allows himself—and others—a moment's relaxation. He admits having been uptight for the last several days, and predicts he "will probably be that way tomorrow. I get this way when I'm trying to concentrate and don't want to be distracted." But for now, he can be at ease. "We had to win," he says. "We just couldn't be number one for only a day." His thoughts ramble on to Saturday's rematch with the Bruins. "We're going to do something different," he says, "something they won't expect. If they think this one is going to be easy, they are in for a surprise."

*  *  *

When I talked to Kansas coach Ted Owens just before the game tonight, he said he appreciated my comment that the UCLA win was for eighty-eight other coaches. Ted lost to the Bruins by eight points in the 1971 national semifinals, so he knows what I was talking about.

Earlier in the season, Ted had asked if we wanted to use the Big Eight's thirty-second clock for this game. I declined, because I knew we wouldn't have enough time after playing UCLA to practice for it. This turned out to be a lucky break for us, since the clock would have made the delay offense impossible to run.

## WEDNESDAY, JANUARY 23

A 5:45 wake-up call rousts the team out of bed and onto the bus for a ride to Kansas City and an early-morning flight back through Chicago to South Bend. The players are tired, but for now, the anxieties of the season are far below them. UCLA is a team they have just beaten, not one they must soon play again. Tomorrow's game against St. Francis of Pennsylvania is a port of refuge. Cued by Phelps, the stewardess announces to the other passengers that the number-one basketball team in the whole country is aboard. Applause at 25,000 feet is exhilarating.

While waiting at O'Hare for the flight connection to South

Bend, Novak asks his teammates to autograph the latest issue of *Sports Illustrated*. The lead story this week is headlined "AFTER 88 COMES ZERO." A four-page color layout isn't enough for Phelps, however, who is miffed that the magazine's annual bathing-suit spread has kept his team off the cover. "The greatest comeback in the history of basketball," he says, "and this is what they choose for their cover."

Conveniently, the afternoon practice is shorter than usual. The team is uninspired, the next opponent is not in Notre Dame's class, and WNDU-TV is rebroadcasting the UCLA game at 6:30.

The players watch on the television sets in their rooms, while the coaches, notebooks in hand, watch in their homes. Sitting in his den, Phelps begins to imagine what it will be like in Los Angeles. He hears the crowd; he sees Wooden shaking his program. And he wonders what to do about it.

Digger does not doubt the ability of his team to play UCLA head-to-head. That has been proved. But there are all those other factors to consider. Since defeating Kansas, he has been struggling with an idea: to substitute Paterno for Novak and run the four-corner delay offense with Dantley controlling the ball. This might be just the way to rattle the Bruins and befuddle Wooden. He considers doing it early, to create three-on-two match-ups underneath, where the Irish are strongest. He calls DiBiaso, and the two share their ideas.

\* \* \*

It's going to take something special to beat UCLA at Pauley Pavilion. A lot of teams lose there before they ever walk onto the court. If we could just get an early lead, and then hold the ball awhile, it would really shake them up. I'm not so much afraid of what UCLA can do to us, as of what the atmosphere can make us do to ourselves.

# THURSDAY, JANUARY 24

Reading through the pile of letters, telegrams, messages, and newspaper clippings that followed the win over UCLA, Phelps laments, "I think I'm going blind."

This afternoon, before the game with St. Francis, the Notre Dame team gathers to discuss UCLA. McLaughlin suggests that special attention be paid to Walton.

"If he keeps getting the ball, he can really hurt us," Frank says. "He might score a hundred points. Shumate can't stop him alone if Walton turns on. Nobody can."

"We aren't going to change our strategy to concentrate on one man," Phelps answers. "We've tried that before, and it doesn't work. Besides, I'm still worried about Wilkes. He wasn't his usual self Saturday, but he will be at home."

McLaughlin then tries a lighter suggestion: "I wonder if Wooden would let us hang in Pauley the nets we cut down Saturday?" Phelps smiles. If only everything could be the same.

"I'll guarantee you one thing," he says firmly. "We'll be ready for them. I don't care if we are fourteen-point underdogs. That's just the way I like it."

Dave Kuzmicz, the freshman from South Bend, comes by McLaughlin's office later. He is troubled because he has appeared in only seven games and has scored only fifteen points. "I know I should be doing better," he says, "and I'd like to be. It's just been hard. I'm not used to playing guard yet."

"Don't worry about it, Kuz," McLaughlin says. "We know it's tough for you, but you're doing fine. Just continue to work at your game. Brokaw and Clay will be gone after next year, and that should open things up some. You're just a freshman."

"Yeah, I guess you're right," he responds. "But I'm glad

about one thing. I may not be playing much, but at least I'm on the number-one team in the country."

Despite Tuesday night's scare against Kansas and St. Francis' 10–5 record, the players consider tonight's game a useless evening's exercise. They are not looking beyond the unheralded eastern team; they are looking through it. "We should blow them out of here," Phelps emphasizes in the dressing room, "but don't let them make up in enthusiasm what they lack in ability. Don't let them get hungry."

Notre Dame jumps out to a 10–2 start, then obligingly lets St. Francis move into the lead. At half time, ahead by only nine points, 41–32, the players sit quietly. They know what to expect when Phelps finishes analyzing the first twenty minutes with his assistants. And Digger doesn't disappoint them. "Where are they ranked, Shu?" he mocks. "Is there something about them I don't know, Adrian? Are you pissed off I took you out of the game, Goose?

"They smell an upset, the greatest win in the history of their school. Be proud of yourselves. You did a great job. I told you not to let their emotion keep them in it. You don't deserve to be number one! If you want to go to the NIT, I'll call and get it for you right away. If you want to be number one for only a day or two, you can have it. I can't believe it! I smelled it all day. I smelled it with your cocky attitude. You asked for it, and you deserve it."

"C'mon, let's go," interjects Clay. "We'll get 'em. We just have to play tougher."

For the second time in three games, Phelps does not start Novak in the second half, going with Paterno instead. The Irish do not play much better, but they are more dedicated. When the 78–58 victory is complete, St. Francis coach Pete Lonergan says of the top-ranked team in the country, "They weren't able to stop anything we tried." Brokaw, whose twelve-point mini-effort was his lowest of the year, says, "I never shoot that well before a big game."

The big game is exactly what Phelps wants to talk about. "I want you to sacrifice the next two days," he tells the team. "When we get to Los Angeles tomorrow, I don't want you to think about the beach, your relatives, or anything except beating UCLA. We're going out there to defend what we've already won. You *are* going to win. Any time you can come back from seventeen points and outscore a team twelve-oh in the last three and a half minutes, you are better than they are. It's ten o'clock now. In exactly twelve hours, we're going to practice for an hour before leaving. The key to this week is rest, so go back to your dorms and get some."

Chris Stevens is in no mood to rest. He won't be going to Los Angeles anyway. He appeared in his sixth game of the year tonight, and scored his third basket—a long jumper that drew unaccustomed cheers. Hawk wants to celebrate with his girl friend at Corby's. He's just about to walk in when Phelps rides by, honks his horn, and waves.

\* \* \*

I have read comments in the newspaper this week suggesting we shouldn't bother going out to play UCLA again. Al McGuire has said, "All Notre Dame did by winning was to guarantee UCLA its eighth straight national championship." Curtis Rowe, one of Wooden's former players, said, "If they expect to win in Los Angeles, they'd better bring some more players."

What are we supposed to do, apologize to them for winning? I didn't know beating UCLA was such a mortal sin. Our victory didn't guarantee anything for the Bruins; it did just the opposite. It proved they can be beaten, that some other team has a chance at the title this year. And as for Rowe's remark, I'd much rather bring different officials than different players.

## FRIDAY, JANUARY 25

Last night's victory over St. Francis, unimpressive as it was, has given Notre Dame a rare distinction. It represents the twenty-third straight victory by the Irish football and basketball teams, a streak unequaled in fifty-eight years. They could take a giant step toward breaking the all-time record of twenty-nine set by Texas A&M in 1919–20 by beating UCLA tomorrow.

The players are eager for the morning workout, since it is the first of the week devoted entirely to the Bruins. "Oh, man, am I ready," Clay says enthusiastically as he jukes down to the auxiliary gym's court. The team goes over the same defensive strategy it used in last Saturday's game. Phelps tells Brokaw to be more aware of Walton's backdoor pass to Trgovich breaking underneath. He reminds Shumate to block Walton off the boards.

Offensively, the team runs through what Digger hopes will be a few unexpected twists designed to create more scoring opportunities for Brokaw and Dantley, and to take advantage of Shumate's outside shooting. "They haven't seen these things," Phelps tells the team, "but it's nothing new to us." Digger doubts that Wooden has made any major adjustments at all.

At one point during practice, Phelps goes over to Stevens, who is sitting on the sideline. "Were you going into Corby's last night, Hawk?"

"Yeah. Why?"

"Forget about dressing the next three home games."

Thirty minutes after practice ends, a police escort hurries Notre Dame to the South Bend airport. Dantley, head back, smiling and with his arms spread across the rear seat of the speeding bus, says, "This is what it's all about, man, the way it ought to be."

The players relax on the flight from Chicago. The blacks play cards in the 747 tourist lounge; the others mostly stay in their seats.

Phelps, in a reflective mood, hides out in a more isolated part of the aircraft. He is the coach of the number-one team in the country and as he talks, that country passes symbolically below him.

"No matter what happens out here tomorrow, nobody can take Saturday's game away from us," he begins. "It was the highlight of the entire college season and, considering the circumstances, one of the greatest comebacks of all time. The point is we beat them, something no one else has been able to do for a long time. I know they can blow us out tomorrow, but that wouldn't get them back their loss. A lot of people are looking at this as if it were a two-game series. That misses the point. No matter what happens here, last Saturday's game stands completely by itself."

Phelps stops to buckle his seat belt when the plane is bounced by turbulence.

"If we lose, it's not the end of the world. We'll still consider ourselves number two, even if no one else does. We could still get one more crack at them in Greensboro."

Digger's thoughts turn to his disrupted home life.

"I miss the family a lot. Even when I was at home the last few weeks, I wasn't really 'there.' I haven't been sleeping very well either. I would give it all up if it were hurting my family. So far, I don't think it has, but it's tough on the kids. The most refreshing thing that's happened to me recently was Karen's coming into the den, and just smiling at me."

Just before the plane lands, Phelps recalls his first trip to play UCLA two years ago right after the 94–29 loss to Indiana. "I bought a newspaper," he says. "On the first page of the sports section was a picture of a gas chamber captioned 'The First Nationally Televised Execution.' I'll never forget that. I never want to forget it."

The team's plane is met by well-wishers and a battery of television cameras. The players share Phelps' concern about such distractions. "This limelight is bad for me, makes me blow my cool," says the Iceman. Crotty frowns and says, "C'mon, Digger. This is bad. Let's get out of here."

In the lobby of the Century Plaza Hotel, Phelps gathers the players before they go to their rooms. "Don't bother to look at the newspapers," he cautions. "There won't be anything worth reading."

Later, everyone goes to Digger's suite to watch the first half of last Saturday's game film. "Don't get discouraged about the officials," he says. "I'll take care of them. You just keep your poise and show your class, no matter what happens on the court. UCLA and their fans want revenge, so the pressure is on them. If you can accept the crowd and UCLA's intensity, we will win again. That is all it takes to shut people up."

The players have been given expense money to eat dinner on their own. Phelps tells them to be in bed by eleven. Most have no place to go and nothing to do, although Novak has brought a few textbooks along. Paterno is mainly interested in the girls and the palm trees mysteriously sprouting right out of the sidewalk. Brokaw visits his mother and father at a nearby Holiday Inn. The police captain and his wife have made the trip as guests of friends back home. "That was really nice," says Brokaw. "I hope it was worth the effort."

At Pauley Pavilion, UCLA is playing its first game since losing to the Irish. Toward the end of the 96–54 win over Santa Clara, the Bruin students start yelling "Beat Notre Dame! Beat Notre Dame! Beat Notre Dame!"

*  *  *

There is not much left to do now, except wait. I only hope we play as well as we can and don't ever fall too far behind. A comeback this week will be difficult.


## SATURDAY, JANUARY 26


From the beginning, it seems that time, place, and circumstance have joined to mock the Notre Dame team. Many of the players, unaccustomed to the time change, awaken two hours early. During the morning shooting practice, they conclude that round arenas like their own are better. The visitors' dressing room is too small, too crowded. The bench area is too far removed from centercourt. Clay is coming down with a cold.

Pauley Pavilion, where UCLA has lost only twice in eight and a half years, is all but empty—yet conspiracy is already in the air. Outside, a few hundred students, many of them holdovers from last night's game, wait to claim good seats when the doors open at 5:30. As the players climb into cabs to return to the hotel, one of the squatters yells out, "Tonight you'll meet your fate."

The players say little as they sit in Phelps' suite watching the second half of last Saturday's game film. The coach emphasizes the need for better rebounding, and the virtues of poise and composure. At the pregame meal, the team feels uncomfortable in the carpeted and chandeliered elegance of the Regents' Board Room. Novak interrupts the nervous quiet: "C'mon, somebody say something to loosen us up." Nobody does.

On this day, nobody can. It is more than the UCLA team; it is the whole panoply of championship banners and pom-pon girls and John Wooden pyramids of success. In the dressing room before the game, there is none of the previous Saturday's easy confidence. "You're better than they are," Phelps pleads. "It's like one neighborhood team going cross-town to play another. Just be ready for what is going to happen when you get out there."

What they hear when they get out there is the ultimate psych—the UCLA cheering section humming the Notre Dame fight song. And they see a banner that reads, "The Lord Giveth, but the Bruins Taketh Away."

UCLA's starting lineup presents another unexpected surprise. Wooden has benched Trgovich, moved Meyers to the left wing, and inserted freshman Marques Johnson at the right wing. But the biggest problem is the awesome presence of Walton.

Although he commits two turnovers and an offensive foul in the first two scoreless minutes, it is obvious that Walton has all the intensity the roaring crowd demands. His first basket comes at 17:56 on a pass from Johnson and sends the Bruins charging to a 9–0 lead. Phelps calls time out, but the game is nearly six minutes old before Dantley's fourteen-foot jumper gives the Irish their first points.

Notre Dame is down 33–17 with 4:43 left when it tries to repeat last week's first-half comeback. The Irish quickly chop the lead to seven points, and Walton goes to the bench with three fouls. But the Bruins outscore them 8–2 in the last two minutes to lead comfortably at half time, 43–30.

UCLA's early performance has been no less sparkling than last week's, and Notre Dame's no better. Wilkes, with eighteen points and eight rebounds, is everything Phelps had feared. Walton, who made all of his seven shots, is everything Mc-

Laughlin had feared. And while the Bruins hit 64 percent from the floor, the Irish make 36.

Notre Dame shoots better in the second half, and Brokaw holds Wilkes to two points after Phelps belatedly switches defensive assignments, but the Irish have no real hope. Walton's assortment of short-range hooks and jumpers, and Johnson's six-inch height advantage over Clay, give UCLA a twenty-eight-point lead with six minutes left.

Seconds later, Walton picks up his fifth foul. Turning to the UCLA bench at the far end of the court, he gives a wave and a smile, and majestically heads for the dressing room. His thirty-two points are a season high for the Bruins, who go on to win 94–75. The once and future kingdom has been restored.

Phelps is a gracious loser when he meets the press. "They played a perfect game," he says with a smile indicating relief that the two-week ordeal is over. "There's not much you can do about that."

Wooden sits by UCLA's dressing room door with his legs crossed, his arms folded, one hand holding his silver cross, and the other an orange drink. "Yes," he admits, "there are times when a loss can help a team."

A few minutes later Wooden walks into the Notre Dame dressing room. He tells Kuzmicz that he coached his father in high school years ago. Kuzmicz seems pleased. He apologizes to Shumate for any bitterness that may have developed between the two teams. Shumate chats respectfully, and calls him "Mr. Wooden."

A few feet away, Clay says softly, "We weren't ready. I don't know what it was, but we just weren't ready."

The ordeal over, the team hurries to the airport to catch the red-eye flight to Chicago. After take-off, the players move to the lounge to flirt with the stewardesses. DiBiaso and Phelps are also up front, smoking long cigars and drinking beer. Everyone is happy, laughing, relaxed. It is an Irish wake.

A bus is waiting at the airport to take the team back to South Bend. When it stops at the Indiana Skyway toll booth near the site of Shumate's accident, Ed O'Rourke, the super-fan, gets off. "How are you getting home from here?" somebody asks. "I don't know," he says in the shivering predawn cold. "I'll figure out something."

The team bus continues on. A few minutes later, one of Mayor Daley's streetcleaners pulls up to the toll booth.

"Which way you headed?" O'Rourke asks the driver.

"Down this way," the driver says, pointing.

"How about a lift?" the lawyer asks.

"Hop in," the driver says.

And that's how Ed O'Rourke makes it from a toll booth on the Indiana Skyway to the South Shore Country Club.

\* \* \*

For the rest of this season I have one goal, to get another shot at UCLA. They've beaten us, but they aren't a better team. We will prove that in Greensboro if we get the chance.

The fact that Wooden changed his attack indicates his respect for us. He would never admit it, of course, but that's exactly what he did.

If anyone thinks UCLA will fall apart when Walton and Wilkes leave, this game certainly proved otherwise. Johnson was super; in fact, UCLA has the best overall freshman talent in the country. The only reason Richard Washington, Gavin Smith, and Jim Spillane don't play is that they aren't needed yet.

Incidentally, the trip ended appropriately enough when I got home and discovered I had claimed the wrong garment bag at the airport.

McLaughlin is up early this morning. While the team was in California, he and Bob Whitmore scouted Marquette's 71–54 win over Loyola in Chicago. Now, he sits at the combination dining and bumper-pool table in his two-bedroom house on Rockne Drive and prepares a comprehensive report on the Warriors.

As a kid, McLaughlin would come down from the Bronx to be Marquette's ballboy when it played in the old Madison Square Garden. But, in basketball years, that was generations ago. Frank has since starred at Fordham Prep—where he won all-city honors along with a tall, skinny kid from Power Memorial named Lew Alcindor—and captained his team at Fordham University. He was a late draft choice of the Knickerbockers in 1969, but no real threat to make the team. After a reserve hitch and a season as an assistant at Holy Cross, he joined up with Phelps at Fordham.

The coaches spend very little time in their postmortem of the UCLA loss. "How did it look on television?" Phelps asks McLaughlin.

"Like we were too hesitant, not moving the ball enough," Frank answers. "And it was obvious that our outside shooting was way off."

Phelps says that if the Irish play UCLA again, Brokaw must guard Wilkes with Paterno or Novak on Johnson. "I suppose we could give Shu some help on Walton, but if we sag, they'll just pop the open shot from outside."

The discussion moves on to the Tuesday game against Marquette. "They don't shoot well from the outside, and they don't try to run," McLaughlin reports. "Their game is quickness, penetration, and hitting the boards. I think a zone might be good."

DiBiaso disagrees. "I don't know, Frank. We might not

execute a zone very well, because we haven't used it in a game yet."

"That doesn't bother me," Phelps interrupts. "Al doesn't have a good zone offense, and he wouldn't be expecting us to run one anyway."

"It could throw them off their game," McLaughlin emphasizes. "We'd just have to hope they didn't get lucky and hit a couple of shots. They're so quick, I don't see how we could press them."

The difference of opinion irritates Phelps. "What the hell's going on? 'We can't press.' 'We can't zone.' Should I call off the game?"

The team practices in the auxiliary gym because an auto show has taken over the main arena. Phelps gathers the players at midcourt to speak of UCLA one last time. "We didn't play our game and they were super inspired to beat us," he says matter-of-factly. "You know what we have to do to get another chance at them. I think the pendulum will swing back our way. You just get to Greensboro and I promise you I'll have a game plan that will beat them."

The players seem relieved that the heavy yoke of national leadership has been removed. After a spirited, enthusiastic workout, Shumate says, "We may have lost Saturday, but there was a prize in that package. We're gonna come back Tuesday."

\* \* \*

The team must be ready for this one, since two consecutive losses would be bad right now. I'm sure Marquette is confident. They think our players are down, and they want to beat us here because we ended their eighty-one-game home winning streak last year. I know just how they'd like to do it too. Marquette will play a slow, deliberate game; work like heck on defense; and hope to beat us something like 52–48.

I can also be sure that Al McGuire will get a technical foul. That's his way of making the referees more conscious of their calls against his team. He'd rather have the crowd coming down on him or the officials than his own players. Al is more than a showman; he's a master of game psychology. The only coach with a record better than his over the last five years is Wooden.

I like Al, like his flamboyance. And I know his methods can work. After I got a technical in our game in Milwaukee last season, we started to cut a big lead. Al called time-out, ran up to the official, and said, "Gimme one. If that's what it takes, I want one too." Al should have known he taught me that trick in the first place. Marquette beat my Fordham team in the Garden three years ago because I let Al control the game by not getting a technical after he did. My game plan now is to get up when he gets up, and yell when he yells. In other words, match him tit for tat and "T" for "T."

## MONDAY, JANUARY 28

Hawk Stevens, grounded by Phelps' three-game suspension, is unhappy. "It wasn't fair," he says before practice. "Digger knew my girl friend's parents were coming in to see me play this week because I asked him for tickets. If I thought he was pissed off when he rode by Corby's the other night, I wouldn't have gone in. He wouldn't have seen me in the first place if I hadn't gone back out to the parking lot to give one of the freshmen my ID card. But I'm the only one he saw. Or I suppose I'm the only one he saw."

He slips on his blue practice-jersey and continues. "I can't understand what the big deal is about anyway. I didn't get drunk and jump up and down on any tables. And he knows some of the players drink. He saw us after games two years ago in motel bars and in our rooms, and didn't say anything about it. If he had to make an example of somebody, it seems he could have found one more worthy of criticism."

Dantley is off his game in practice today and Bob Whitmore is concerned about him. "A. D. called me last night," Bob says. "He said he wasn't sure about when to shoot. I told him to play like I did: 'When you have it, take it.' "

Sitting up in the stands is an NBA scout interested in Shumate. "Shumate should stay one more year," the man observes. "I doubt he'll go real high in the draft because he hasn't proven he can play forward."

\* \* \*

Terry and I had dinner with the Keiths tonight. Larry's wife, Carolyn, has flown in to see the Marquette game and spend a few days with him. This makes Jennifer happy because, with Larry in a motel now, she can have her room back.

## TUESDAY, JANUARY 29

UCLA has retaken its familiar place at the head of the latest wire-service polls, while Notre Dame has slipped to third behind North Carolina State. Dave Israel of the Chicago *Daily News* refused to let the Bruins' takeover be unanimous by casting his first-place vote for the Irish. Marquette is fifth.

Al McGuire is as relaxed in his approach to basketball as Phelps is intense. Forty-five minutes before tip-off, while Phelps is furiously writing his game plan on the dressing-room blackboard, the affable Marquette coach is having a drink with friends.

"What time is it?" McGuire casually inquires.

"Seven fifteen," he is told.

"I guess I should go then. I promised a reporter I'd talk to him before the game."

In the Notre Dame dressing room, Phelps is at an emotional peak. "We need this one," he begins. "You're now third in the country because of the way you played against UCLA. We've got to have that one out of our system. Do we want to go back to the NIT? I don't think so."

The more he talks, the more intense he becomes, until finally he is blistering, raging, summoning Rockne-esque visions of team pride, school pride, self-pride. "They want you," he says, looking into the eyes of every player. "You better want them. You better want to go back up in the polls. If you don't feel that way, your ass will be on the bench."

As the players charge out ahead of the coaches, DiBiaso says to Phelps, "For a while there, I wondered if you were okay."

Referee Art White has a pretty good idea of what he is in for tonight. Before the tip-off, he makes note of last night's Ali-Frazier bout and says to Digger, "Just remember the fight was last night."

Meanwhile, on press row, reporters are getting up a pool to predict when McGuire will receive his first technical.

The writers don't have to wait long to declare a winner. The game is tied 2–2 when a foul called on Marcus Washington catapults McGuire off the bench. Al has his technical with exactly one minute gone.

McGuire's eruption does not deter Notre Dame from a

sparkling first-half performance. Though Marquette forces the slow pace Phelps expected, the Irish take a 33–25 lead into the locker room by hitting 61 percent of their shots. Marquette can make only 38 percent.

The Warriors turn the game around in the second half on scoring by forward Bo Ellis and guard Lloyd Walton. Ellis pours in ten points against three different defenders, and Walton drives past Clay for six as Marquette surges into the lead.

The Irish are trailing 45–43 with 10:19 left, when a foul on Martin gives Phelps the opportunity he wanted. He hollers. He waves his arms. He stomps around. He fumes. And he gets his technical foul. After Ellis sinks the free throw, the harangue pays a dividend of nine straight points that put the Irish back into control.

The comeback begins when Ellis picks up his fourth foul and goes to the bench. He does not return until Clay's twenty-footer from the corner has given the Irish a 52–46 lead with 6:53 left. Ellis scores only one more basket before fouling out four minutes later. With the freshman forward gone and Washington, Walton, and Earl Tatum saddled with four fouls each, the Warriors look to center Maurice Lucas for help. But Lucas is in the throes of a three-for-sixteen shooting night and isn't much help.

Notre Dame wins 69–63, despite squandering eleven of its twenty-four free-throw opportunities. Shumate's twenty-seven points and Paterno's fourteen offset disappointing performances by Brokaw and Dantley, who combine for only sixteen points, seventeen below their collective average. "They put a lot of pressure on me," Brokaw says, "but if they had known I had a cold, they probably wouldn't have wasted their time." Dantley also has a cold, and he's been dieting to lose weight.

Phelps is overjoyed by the win and generous with his praise. "You showed class tonight," he tells the team with enthusiasm that belies his weariness. "I'm really proud of you. You showed you belong in the NCAA tournament. You beat a good team. Some of you didn't play well, but don't worry about it. The game's over, so forget it."

McGuire is the same composed, soft-spoken self he is before and after any game. A parting shot at the officials? Not from Al. "I thought the officiating was good throughout the entire game," he says. "They've got a tough job."

\* \* \*

This one took a lot out of me. I delayed the post-game press conference until all the writers arrived, because I was too tired to say anything twice.

It's a circus when Marquette plays Notre Dame, and Al and I are always in the center ring. From what I could tell, there was a lot going on in the stands as well. While we were warming up before the second half, I saw what looked to be a Notre Dame student wearing a leprechaun's costume. Then he tore off his suit, jumped up on some beefy guy's shoulders, and flashed a T-shirt that read "Marquette." Now that's what I call school spirit, especially since he was surrounded by eleven thousand Notre Dame fans.

## WEDNESDAY, JANUARY 30

Phelps learns this morning that while his basketball team was gaining a victory, his television show was losing a sponsor. During the night, King's Palace burned down.

There is no staff meeting to discuss either last night's game or tomorrow's against DePaul. McLaughlin is handling the preparation for the Blue Demons himself. Phelps' main business of the day is administrative. He and Parseghian meet with Fr. Joyce to discuss better methods of preparing freshman athletes for college academics. Later, he receives a copy of the proposed budget for next season's basketball program. Five percent more money has been allocated for operational expenses, but due to an oversight by Phelps, nothing has been included for new uniforms. Digger will bring the matter up with Krause later.

\* \* \*

I got my reward for beating Marquette today—a genuine Milwaukee sausage hand-delivered by Peggy Schumaker, seventeen-year-old daughter of a Notre Dame alumnus. I sent her tickets to the game after she wrote me a three-page letter in November: "I want Notre Dame fans, alumni and students all over the country victoriously singing the Notre Dame Fight Song for weeks after the [Marquette] game. Let's continue on in the spirit of Rockne, to fight and win no matter how great the odds. . . . Let us silence the Marquette battle cry with the roar of the Notre Dame Fight Song, once and for all!"

I've got to admit I'm partial to that sort of talk.

## THURSDAY, JANUARY 31

Del Harris, coach at Earlham College in Richmond, Indiana, is in Phelps' office to discuss his book *Multiple Defense for Winning Basketball.* As Harris fills a blackboard with one diagram after another, it becomes obvious that Digger's primary interest is finding a defense to stop UCLA. "We can't match-up press them," he admits. "I'd love to come up with some other defense to beat them. What kind of halfcourt pressure do you recommend against a one-guard offense?"

The two men examine various strategies until the telephone rings. The call is from an Atlanta consulting firm which represents a college interested in building a basketball program. The caller refuses to disclose the school, but he does say that "money is no object."

"The first problem," Phelps replies, "would be hiring a good coach. I doubt many major-college coaches would be willing to move into such an uncertain situation. But an assistant coach or a small-college coach might."

The man asks Digger if he would be interested, anyway.

"I've built two programs from scratch," he answers. "I'm not going to try to do it again."

Phelps advises that "instant success" in major-college basketball can often be traced to "cheating and very low academic standards." Otherwise, he tells the consultant, "it takes a long time."

After so many difficult games in recent days, Phelps hopes DePaul can be dispatched early—and easily. "For once," he tells the team before the game, "I'd love to blow somebody out in a hurry. Let's give everyone a chance to play."

The latter prospect is especially appealing to Crotty, who has appeared in only four of the seven January games, scoring three points. "Yeah," he interrupts with a laugh, "that's the idea."

This doesn't appear to be that kind of contest, however. The Irish lead early, then fall behind midway through the period, finishing the half with an uncertain 43–40 lead.

It is not that Notre Dame has played so badly. DePaul, 10–7 and coached for the thirty-second year by Irish alumnus Ray Meyer, has played well.

After action resumes, Notre Dame finally breaks the game open by outscoring the Blue Demons 23–6 in the first seven and a half minutes. Phelps begins substituting two minutes later, and the first person off the bench is Crotty.

Though Peter is satisfied to merely be in the game, Dantley's pleasure comes from ending his recent slump. After popping a long jumper midway through the period, Adrian punctuates his obvious return to form with a wide grin and an upraised fist.

Dantley finally goes to the bench at 4:34, after a twenty-seven-minute performance which produced his best totals of the year: 23 points and 15 rebounds. A minute and a half later DePaul, trailing 93–72, asks for time-out.

While the Notre Dame students call for the popular Ken Wolbeck with cheers of "Geek! Geek!" the Irish bench rises to greet the players coming off the floor. Crotty is straining to hear Phelps over the noise when he notices Dantley clutching at his shoulder. He thinks his teammate must be "kidding around" when suddenly Adrian drops unconscious to the floor.

Crotty pushes the other players back and grabs for Digger, who quickly orders trainer Arno Zoske to find a doctor. Few people notice what's happened until Phelps runs onto the court and tries to quiet the crowd by waving his arms. Within moments Adrian, still lying motionless, is surrounded by three doctors who can do little more than check his pulse, give him smelling salts, and call for a stretcher. As Dantley is carried away to await an ambulance, Shumate walks alongside.

The Irish dressing room is unusually quiet after the team's 101–72 victory. Brokaw, whose twenty-five points have won him a second Wendell Smith Award as the game's most outstanding player, shakes his head and says, "Boy, that was something."

Phelps, obviously upset, tells the team, "If you ever have

something wrong with you, let us know. That's what we're here for."

After being told that Adrian was conscious and showing "good vital signs" when the ambulance took him to the infirmary, Digger goes to his office to call Mrs. Dantley in Washington. He first explains what has happened and then puts Shumate on. "Don't worry, Mrs. Dantley," John assures her. "We'll take care of Adrian." After they hang up, Phelps says, "When I looked down and saw him on the floor, I nearly died. You can blame the freshman rule for this."

An examination at the infirmary determines that Dantley is suffering from physical exhaustion. His condition, already weakened by his cold, self-imposed diet, and recent lack of sleep, was compounded by the physical activity and excitement of tonight's game. A more definite diagnosis will be available tomorrow when test results can be studied.

\* \* \*

Adrian has so much pride that he keeps a lot of things bottled up inside. He hadn't been playing well lately, and he didn't know exactly what to do about it. I tried to tell him a couple of days ago that he was in a slump, just like the ones baseball players can have, but he wanted to fight it alone.

Considering what happened to Adrian, it seems ironic that Terry and I met Dr. Feodor Lynen at the Faculty Club after the game tonight. He is a guest lecturer who shared the 1964 Nobel Prize for Medicine and Physiology, and he was very interested in Adrian's condition. Terry tells me I referred a few times to the Nobel "Peace Prize"; I hope I didn't insult him.

# FRIDAY, FEBRUARY 1

The coaches' meeting covers tomorrow's game with Davidson College, a Southern Conference school near Charlotte, North Carolina. The Wildcats have won six of their last seven games, including victories over Furman and South Carolina, and they rank second nationally in field-goal shooting, with a 52.6 percentage. The Irish are right behind at 52.4.

Phelps learns in the afternoon that Dantley needs only a few days' rest before he can play again. Understandably, Paterno shows no sense of accomplishment when he learns he will be starting in Adrian's place.

"I haven't earned it," he says. "I still consider myself a substitute."

* * *

I got a call tonight from a player on a team in the South—coincidentally in Davidson's conference—who wants to transfer to Notre Dame. I know the kid because I tried to recruit him, but I had to tell him we don't accept transfers from either junior colleges or four-year schools. I feel we owe this to the players who have made the full four-year commitment to Notre Dame. Besides, any player who is unhappy at one school might just as easily be unhappy here.

# SATURDAY, FEBRUARY 2

Dantley is out of the infirmary and will be wearing street clothes as he sits on the bench during this afternoon's regionally televised game.

"I'm glad to be away from that place," Adrian says, as his teammates suit up around him. "I was the only person in a large room, and last night I dreamed somebody was coming to get me."

Spectators are aware of only half the entertainment available at a game. Unknown to them is the frenzied activity that takes place on the bench—the exhortations of encouragement and lamentations of despair which follow the ebb and flow of battle.

The game is two minutes old when Brokaw hits one of two free throws to put the Irish in front 3–2. "We should be ahead ten-two by now," Phelps mutters angrily. But when a TV time-out is called with the Irish trailing 4–3 a half minute later, Digger tells the players, "Let's relax. Just keep playing. Stay with it and don't worry about it."

When play resumes, Novak lets a pass slip through his hands for the second time and Digger hurries Crotty into the game. Paterno is chastened as he passes the bench for not staying with his man on defense. The Irish are down 10–7 with 6:09 gone, when Digger follows DiBiaso's advice to call a time-out.

There is a flurry of activity during the break, as the managers hand out towels and squeezeable plastic water bottles. Phelps always wants one within easy reach under his chair.

Despite pleas from Kuzmicz for "spurt time," his teammates can do no better than exchange the lead with Davidson. Phelps has Clay and Brokaw switch assignments when Gary's man hits two consecutive outside shots.

Following the defensive change, Notre Dame reels off ten unanswered points to take a 33–22 lead. Novak soon makes the score 37–28 with his first two free throws of the season after twelve straight misses. Clay, on the bench at the moment, says, "He's got the feel now."

When Dwight's replacement, Martin, has trouble getting the ball inside to Shumate, Digger yells out, "Run the damn offense, Martin, and run it right." The half ends with Notre Dame ahead 45–32.

Paterno is due at the free-throw line early in the second half, when another television time-out interrupts play. Digger yells over to the announcing crew, "I'll give you your forty thousand dollars. Just let us play." To the team he says, "Let's get aggressive and play the way we want to."

Less than a minute later, the ball goes out of bounds in front of the Notre Dame bench, and Davidson takes over. Bob Whitmore, who is keeping a statistical chart, tells the referee, "You didn't even see the play."

Without turning around, the referee answers, "You're right, I didn't."

A few minutes later, Phelps loudly informs the officials that "Number fifty is beating the crap out of Paterno in there." He tells Clay not to dribble so close to Shumate before passing him the ball.

Notre Dame is leading 63–46 with 12:31 left when Paterno is benched with his fourth foul. "If you can reach in with your hand," Phelps welcomes him, "why can't you step in with your body to take the offensive foul?"

Back on the court, Shumate has fallen down after a tussle under the basket. It's his Redd Foxx routine and the players on the sideline laugh. As Shu gets up slowly, shaking his head, the crowd laughs too and he seems to enjoy the attention.

The Irish go ahead by twenty after Clay hits four long

jumpers in a row. "What's gotten into Dwight?" Phelps asks. "His girl friend's in town," Martin grins, "and he's putting on a show for her."

The Irish are still comfortably ahead when time is called at 9:22. Lacking anything else to say, Phelps tells the team, "Our foul shooting will cost us the national championship. We don't concentrate. We don't work on it. I guarantee you, it will cost us the national championship." Play resumes, and Shumate sinks two free throws to make the score 76–56.

In the next two minutes, Davidson outscores the Irish six to two and Phelps calls time-out. He emphasizes, "This game isn't over yet. You've got to work. There's plenty of time left for them."

And so there is. The Wildcats run up six more points to bring Phelps leaping off the bench. "CAN WE RUN THE OFFENSE?" he hollers. At 5:32, with the lead cut to ten points, he calls another time-out. "You thought it was over, didn't you?" he shouts. "I warned you this would happen. Now don't be conservative. Be aggressive."

The Irish regain their poise, and while Digger frantically shouts for the four corners with 1:36 left, Novak lets a hook shot fly to put the team up by ten. The final score is 95–84.

Phelps is unhappy in the dressing room because he believes Shumate was clowning several times during the game. Such displays—especially on television—are bad for the Notre Dame image, he feels.

"You're getting to be a real hot dog, Shumate," Digger says angrily. "Well, you can cut it out right now. As long as I'm coach, that's not going to happen."

Digger tells the team that these actions are "bush" and that they should not only win, but win with class. "If there's any celebrating to do, we'll do it in Greensboro."

After calming down, Phelps calls Shumate into a small room off the main dressing area. John, however, is the angry one now. Digger offers to slap five with him, but John refuses to hold out his hand. In fact, as Digger tries to ease the tension, Shumate refuses to say anything.

Only later does John open up. "I didn't say anything," he tells a friend, "because I was afraid I might say something I'd regret. I wasn't cutting up out there. I just couldn't help laughing when the crowd started doing it. I knew Digger would be mad and would say something about it, but I didn't expect him to embarrass me in front of my teammates. This is one time I don't respect his decision."

Meanwhile, Phelps has hurried home to watch Michigan State—Monday's opponent in East Lansing—play Purdue on television. The Spartans pull a 76–74 upset.

\* \* \*

Now that we're 15–1, I'm confident we will get the NCAA bid I've wanted all season. We may still lose a few more games, but we've proven we're a tournament team. I don't want the players to let down in any way, but I personally feel we have locked up the bid.

## SUNDAY, FEBRUARY 3

As the Irish prepare to play Michigan State, Gary Novak can't help relishing his performance against Davidson. It was by far his best effort of the year and it followed a six-game dry spell in which he had scored only twenty points. His output against Davidson included seventeen points (on seven-for-eight field-goal attempts and three-for-five free throws), six rebounds, and seven assists. The best part of all, though, was making those foul shots.

"It was really beginning to bug me," he says before practice. "I started thinking more about the ones I missed than the ones I should be trying to make. After a while, it got to be funny in a way. It really had me ticked off."

\* \* \*

Goose is always more effective when he isn't overmatched. That's why he didn't surprise me yesterday. A coach can be fairest in his judgments if he knows exactly what each player's capabilities are.

## MONDAY, FEBRUARY 4

On the bus ride to East Lansing this morning, DiBiaso asks Dantley how he feels.

"I'm okay," he answers with characteristic succinctness.

The coaches realize, however, that most college athletes are reluctant to admit physical disability. The demand to "tough it out" only partially explains their hesitance; no less important is a player's own desire to play and not sit on the bench.

Myron Schuckman, for example, takes two aspirin before practice every day to ease the pain in his knees. At the moment, he is recovering from an elbow to the eye which causes double vision "whenever I look up at the basket."

Four straight conference wins have put Michigan State in the thick of the Big Ten race and whetted the home crowd's appetite for the third-ranked Irish. The Spartans jet out to a 12–2 lead and sixteen minutes later, Shumate's lay-up breaks the game's seventh tie and puts the Irish ahead for the first time, 38–36. After four more minutes and one technical foul by Phelps, Notre Dame goes to the dressing room with the lead, 43–39.

It has been a rough contest, but a good one, with the Irish shooting 61 percent and Michigan State 55 percent. Shumate and Novak gave the half added significance when they became the sixteenth and seventeenth Notre Dame players to register one thousand points in a career. Shumate's accomplishment is especially impressive, since only four other players made it in their junior seasons.

The battle continues to rage close in the second half, as both teams sharpen their already deadly marksmanship. With 2:42 remaining, the Spartans inch ahead by four on Terry Furlow's driving hook. Sixteen seconds later Brokaw deposits two free throws to make it 89–87. After Mike Robinson commits an offensive foul, Shumate moves inside to tie the score.

Michigan State takes possession and calls two time-outs in the next forty-one seconds, the last with 0:21 remaining. In a similar situation two days ago, the Spartans defeated Purdue on a basket by Mike Robinson. He already has thirty-one points and the Irish expect the Big Ten's two-time leading scorer to go for the winner again.

It is quite a surprise to both teams when Terry Furlow shoots from beyond the top of the key with twelve seconds remaining. The shot misses rim, net, and everything else, and the Irish take over.

Instead of calling time-out, Notre Dame moves up the floor. Paterno fights off a defender by reversing his dribble and discovers Shumate covered in the middle and Clay shut off from doing his Iceman act. On his own now, and with three seconds showing, he launches a nineteen-footer from left of the foul circle which falls sweetly through. Notre Dame wins 91–89.

When word of the team's sixteenth victory in seventeen

games appears on the national wire-service machines, a New Jersey newspaperman calls the Paterno home in Lincroft. It is very late when the writer tells Bill's father he has some news about his son.

For an instant, Mr. Paterno fears that the news is bad.

\* \* \*

This was a typically rough Big Ten game. There were thirty-two fouls called—eighteen on them, fourteen on us—and there could have been a lot more. I don't think I've seen many games in which both teams shot so well. They made 59 percent and we made 63. Adrian was a little off, but that was to be expected. Even so, he scored fifteen points, led our rebounding with nine, and played all but four and a half minutes.

We're four-for-four against the Big Ten now, but three of the games have been very tight. Winning the close ones is something we had trouble doing last year.

## TUESDAY, FEBRUARY 5

Notre Dame flies to Philadelphia this afternoon for tomorrow's LaSalle game. It is a trip Digger looks forward to every year.

No cheap shots at the City of Brotherly Love for him. He cut his teeth on those fratricidal Big Five games among LaSalle, St. Joseph's, Villanova, Temple, and Penn. That dim, creaking piece of basketball antiquity, called the Palestra, is where he was baptized. The Philly fans and press made him tough. And his association with Dick Harter gave him an early taste of national prominence.

*   *   *

I love the atmosphere that surrounds college basketball in Philadelphia. I love the intensity and the competitiveness and the pride. It always disappointed me that there was so little of this among the schools in New York.

When I left Philadelphia, I could look back on a lot of good experiences; fortunately, nothing has happened since to sour me. One of my all-time thrills as a coach occurred when Fordham played PMC Colleges (now Widener College) as part of a Palestra doubleheader. Not only did we win, but I was greeted by a big "Welcome Home" sign and a standing ovation. It shook me up.

The next year, Notre Dame came to town with a 3–13 record, but we played like world-beaters and upset LaSalle 97–71. Last year, we beat Villanova here.

This place has been good to me. I have a lot of friends in Pennsylvania, but I wasn't able to do much socializing tonight. I spent the evening at a nearby high school basketball game watching Dave Batton, one of our top prospects, play.

## WEDNESDAY, FEBRUARY 6

The trip East is not just a homecoming for Phelps. The Shumates, Dantleys, Clays, Paternos, and Martins will all be represented in the Palestra stands tonight. Digger's own contingent includes his parents, his sister, Diane, and her husband, Kirk Nelson.

After the pregame Mass, Fr. Riehle interests Clay in a cold-prevention method guaranteed not to be found at any pharmaceutical counter. Dwight says he'll try it because "I'm a cautious, careful person." Fr. Riehle crosses two candles, holds them against Clay's throat, and recites a blessing. To Dwight, it's just one more example of the "holy moly" at Notre Dame.

The team arrives at the Palestra while Villanova is playing South Carolina. Although the Irish will face both teams later on, Digger is too busy talking to old friends to pay much attention. Shumate would like to watch, but his eye-catching red fedora makes him an easy target for autograph-seekers. "Things start to bother me after a while," John says to someone standing nearby. "The travel, the books, the hostile crowds are irritating. I don't mind signing the autographs, but people don't understand that I'd like to watch the game too."

Shumate may also be irritable because of comments recently made by LaSalle's Joe Bryant. The Explorers' leading scorer and rebounder remembers John from playground games as a bully. Asked about the characterization, John says, "Anything anybody wants to say is okay with me. I don't pay any attention. I'll just go out and play the game. I don't really recollect who he is, anyway. I don't remember them as individuals unless they beat me."

The trip to Philadelphia has calmed Digger's dressing-room demeanor. "This is another game against a team you can beat," he assures the players. "The Villanova and LaSalle students will boo you, but that's what the Big Five is all about. It won't be anything you haven't already seen."

When they return from their pregame warm-up, Phelps reminds them, "Your families came to see you win."

The Irish are their usual dominating selves in the first half, rushing to a 48–33 lead. Digger's half-time message is, "You're doing a real good job, but remember we did the same thing at Kansas and they came back."

So, too, does LaSalle, despite Bryant's being sent to the hospital six minutes into the period after aggravating a bad ankle in a collision with Shumate. Looking like anything but a 12–7 team missing its best player, the Explorers cut a twenty-one point lead to ten, 74–64, with 7:28 remaining. The Irish stiffen, however, even while Dantley fouls out and Clay suffers an ankle injury of his own. They win 98–78.

Brokaw, at his slithery best, has scored a season-high twenty-eight points. "Bizarre, unusual plays," LaSalle coach Paul Westhead calls them afterwards. "My job," Gary's defender adds, "was to get him off balance when he was shooting his jumper. But he does it that way anyway."

In the Notre Dame dressing room, Clay is off in a corner having his sprained left ankle tended to as Phelps tells the team, "You have a day off tomorrow, but go to your classes."

From somewhere in the crowd, Toby Knight's voice is heard. "If we have to go to class, it's not a day off."

\* \* \*

We played well tonight—keeping all the friends and relatives happy—but we should never have let the game get so close in the second half. We seem to lack the killer instinct that enables a team to put the game away early and keep it put away. The one encouraging thing was our free-throw shooting—we were twenty-six for thirty-two, and 80 percent accuracy isn't bad for a team averaging 70.

# THURSDAY, FEBRUARY 7

It's a day of rest for the Irish and their hottest player of late, Gary Brokaw. The last four games have been Magic's best of the year offensively. Since that sparse nine-point effort against Marquette, he has been on a 24.5-point-per-game binge. He's not just shooting more, he's shooting better (65 percent) and handing out more assists (22).

With the season going so well for him and the team, Brokaw has begun to look optimistically to the future. The NCAA tournament is in "the back of my mind," with a possible professional career increasingly in the forefront.

"I think I could step right into pro ball," he says. "This is what I've wanted since I was six years old, and I think I'm near that goal right now."

Brokaw believes there are several reasons why he's playing better this year. Over the summer, he worked hard on his ball-handling and shooting, and built up his arms and wrists in a weight-training program.

"I'm concentrating more on my shots, and I know better when to take them," he adds. "There's not as much pressure on me to score this year; that helps, too. I'm reaching my peak and playing with more confidence."

\* \* \*

Gary is playing well now, but leaving school early to turn pro would be a big mistake. First of all, unlike Shumate, he wouldn't have a degree. My feelings on that point are very strong. Secondly, his dollar value would certainly increase if he waited. Who knows how much better he will be next year? Gary has tremendous ability, to be sure, but he's still very inconsistent. He may have scored ninety-eight points the last four games, but in the previous four he scored forty-nine. He shouldn't over-look that.

## FRIDAY, FEBRUARY 8

The Irish are taking only one day to get ready for Duke, the once-princely Atlantic Coast Conference power which has fallen on hard times. The Blue Devils were 12–14 last season, their first losing record in thirty-five years. They arrive in South Bend today with an 8–10 record and a load of frustration. While trying to notch the school's thousandth all-time victory, they've lost three straight games. The odds do not favor their chances against Notre Dame either, although Duke has never lost to the Irish in five previous meetings.

\* \* \*

Duke is the victim of all the things I dislike about conferences. The ACC is a seven-team league, and three of those teams are in the Top 10. North Carolina State is second, North Carolina is fourth, and Maryland is seventh. Where does that leave a team like Duke, which is trying to rebuild its program? Or other teams with good coaches and players like Wake Forest and Clemson, who are condemned to the second division because of that logjam at the top? As for Virginia, I don't see how my friend, Bill Gibson, can last much longer there. He has had some good seasons, but he never could break past the super teams that have a lock on the conference.

The smartest move South Carolina ever made was pulling out of the ACC to free itself for at-large tournament bids.

I'm familiar with North Carolina State, North Carolina, and Maryland because I recruit against them. We get an Adrian Dantley, they get a Tom LaGarde. North Carolina beat us two years ago in the regular season, we beat them in the NIT a year later. Next year, we play Maryland. It's possible we could face North Carolina State in the tournament.

Duke's problems are the very reasons I prefer coaching an independent team. Notre Dame can lose four or five games and still get a tournament bid. We aren't burdened by the hatred and bitterness that develops between conference rivals. We can pretty much play whom we want and where we want. Conferences are cutthroat and the biggest cutthroat conference of them all is the ACC.

## SATURDAY, FEBRUARY 9

Duke opens in a zone and catches Notre Dame with a cold shooting hand. Ten minutes pass before the Irish can go ahead to stay, ironically on consecutive outside shots by Paterno from twenty-two feet, and Brokaw from twenty-two and twenty. Notre Dame leads 39–27 at intermission by scoring the last ten points of the period.

The Irish concentrate on their inside game in the second half and it pays off with six three-point plays, three by Dantley and one each by Brokaw, Paterno, and Shumate.

The one disappointment in the 87–68 victory is the ineffectiveness of Clay. After limping off the bench early in the game, Dwight can do no better than hobble around for two minutes before he has to sit down again. His bad ankle isn't ready yet.

\* \* \*

Despite shooting poorly against the zone today, we managed big offensive bursts that could have beaten any team. We also rebounded well and held their leading scorer to two points. We're 18–1 because we know there is more than one way to win a game.

Terry and I saw *Serpico* tonight, just the movie to get me in the proper mood for our game in New York City next week.

### SUNDAY, FEBRUARY 10

While Notre Dame's players take the day off, Phelps attends a coaches' convention in upstate New York. The business at hand is one Chris Patton, and the interested parties represent ten different schools, including four presently found in the Top 20.

\* \* \*

Since Shumate has only one more year at the most, our main recruiting objective is a big man. Of the four leading prospects—Rick Robey, Chris Patton, Dave Batton, and Mark Olberding—Olberding seems most likely to help us immediately. On that basis, he is our first choice, but we'd be pleased with any one of them. I also like Batton a lot, but his coach won't let us make personal contact with him until his season ends.

## MONDAY, FEBRUARY 11

In 1971, Digger Phelps and his Fordham Rams were acclaimed from the nosebleed seats at Madison Square Garden to the marble steps of City Hall. Their 26–3 record represented the most wins and fewest losses by a local team in thirty-four years. Fordham was, in fact, the only one of New York's six major colleges to achieve a better record in 1971 than it had in 1970.

By filling the Garden, Phelps' team proved that the college game had not died in the nation's largest city, after all. The point-shaving scandals of two decades past were forgotten. The underground railroad which carries away the area's best high school players seemed less imposing. The New York Knicks could have their first NBA title ever; the college game and the pro game would coexist.

When Phelps packed off to South Bend, some saw all those hopes and dreams going with him. He had run out on his contract, they said, leaving New York no better off in college basketball than a YMCA in St. Petersburg.

Digger is back in New York City today, to attend the weekly meeting of the Metropolitan Basketball Writers Association, and to perform such other promotional chores as will stir up interest in Thursday's game with Fordham. Hal Wissel, Digger's successor on Rose Hill, stands up at the luncheon to comment, "A lot of things were said about Digger leaving Fordham, but that's all in the past."

Phelps' remarks are those of the cautious diplomat: "It's great to be back in New York. College basketball started here with guys like Clair Bee and Nat Holman. . . . I'm very proud to see that the Coach's Association is coming through for [the ailing former Pratt coach] Pic Picariello. I don't think we can do enough for him. . . . It's good to see Louie [Carnesecca] back in college basketball. . . . You deserve to keep the local high school players here, but we hope to get them too. . . . I've got to be a fool to tell you I'm a helluva coach. Without those three freshmen, we wouldn't be where we are. . . . College basketball *is* New York."

Not very scintillating copy, but Digger is in no position to stir up old feelings. That is what some of the reporters want, of course. Marv Albert of WNBC reminds Phelps in a television interview that he has lost twice to Fordham since moving to Notre Dame. Would he like to "crunch, wallop" his old team? Digger refuses to bite. Nor does he respond when Albert asks about the animosity some Fordham people still feel for him.

When the interviews are over, Phelps meets with Madison Square Garden executive Ned Irish. The Garden management would like Notre Dame to play more often in New York, but Phelps is unwilling to sacrifice another home date unless lucrative financial guarantees are made. No agreement is reached, and later Phelps complains, "Notre Dame doesn't need Fordham or Manhattan to draw crowds and make money. We have our own following here and we should be paid accordingly."

\* \* \*

With apologies to Marv Albert, there were some subjects I didn't mind discussing today. One was the problem of freshman eligibility. Another was the need to revitalize college basketball in New York.

The fault, as I see it, should be shared by the schools, the press, and Madison Square Garden. Now that NYU is no longer playing ball—a real tragedy in itself, since its potential always seemed so great—five majors remain active in the city: St. John's, Manhattan, Columbia, Long Island University, and Fordham. These schools should put their differences aside and take advantage of their natural rivalry, as Philadelphia's Big Five has. Incredibly, Manhattan, St. John's, and Columbia each play only one other school in New York's "Big Five"—Fordham—while LIU plays none. They should be meeting each other twice a year.

The New York media could help the situation by paying more attention to its own teams, players, and coaches. The proportion of college coverage to professional coverage is way out of line.

Finally, and maybe most important of all, ticket prices at the Garden should be lowered. These days, the average fan can't afford to come into the city, park his car, and watch a game. The Garden would do better in the long run to lower its prices in order to increase its potential audience. Create the demand, and the profit margin will take care of itself—or so they taught me at Rider.

New York's potential for college basketball is the best in the country, if everyone involved would just take advantage of it.

## TUESDAY, FEBRUARY 12

With Phelps back in South Bend, Notre Dame begins preparing for Fordham. A win over the young Rams would fulfill one of the season's secondary goals. Every team which defeated Notre Dame last year has been beaten in this season's rematch: Ohio State, St. Louis, Indiana, Kentucky, UCLA, and Duke. Fordham, only 6–13, should be next.

\* \* \*

Terry and I went to a cocktail party tonight for the writers who are conducting a campus workshop. When Bruce Jay Friedman told Terry, "I bet you were a cheerleader," my liberated wife replied, "Bullshit, Friedman."

## WEDNESDAY, FEBRUARY 13

Airplane troubles delay Notre Dame's arrival at LaGuardia by three hours. This is particularly upsetting to the players, since seven members of the twelve-man traveling squad are from the metropolitan area.

Phelps drops his bags at the Statler Hilton and hurries to meet some friends at an Italian restaurant on the West Side. During dinner, McLaughlin is asked his feelings about playing Fordham. "Nothing special," the alumnus says. "I want to beat them tomorrow, and I hope they do well the rest of the season."

\* \* \*

Fr . Riehle was exposed to an unfortunate bit of local color tonight. On the way to the restaurant, we passed a girl lying on the sidewalk in front of a bar. She was neither hurt nor ill, but Fr. Riehle seemed put off by the whole scene. "Father," I said, "welcome to New York."

## THURSDAY, FEBRUARY 14

Notre Dame's appearance in tonight's doubleheader has attracted 14,682 people, the largest regular-season college crowd at the Garden since Fordham's 1971 appearance against Marquette. In the dressing room, Digger assures the players, "This is *our* crowd. They came out to see you. Fordham didn't get them here."

The players receive an enthusiastic reception as they walk onto the court, but Phelps' introduction is greeted by a smattering of boos and obscene signs.

The Irish move out to a 46–31 half-time lead by making 63 percent of their shots, but in the second half, they cool considerably. After going ahead 72–55 with 6:42 remaining, Notre Dame does not score another field goal, though it still manages to win 79–69. Dantley leads the way with his second straight twenty-seven-point game on a fine eleven-for-fourteen shooting performance.

Phelps is more concerned with his team's physical condition after the game than anything else. It was a one-sided brawl in which Fordham committed twenty-two fouls, enabling Notre Dame to sink twenty-one of thirty-three free throws. Clay, still hobbling, saw limited action, and now Shumate is limping with a banged-up knee. "They were overt," Brokaw says in the dressing room, gingerly touching the stitch that was needed on the cut over his eye.

This was the third straight game we didn't play our best, but that doesn't matter. We won by 10. How many are we supposed to win by? We're 20–1 now and the important thing is to get ready for South Carolina.

After the game, I ran into Bill Mainor, one of my Fordham players. It was good to see him again. As long as I have a good relationship with those guys, I'll never be bothered by what anyone else says or does. As far as I'm concerned, people should let the Phelps-Fordham controversy die once and for all.

## FRIDAY, FEBRUARY 15

Notre Dame flies directly to Columbia, where the four-teenth-ranked Gamecocks await with a 17–3 record and a thirty-four-game home winning streak on the Tartan floor of Carolina Coliseum.

The Irish spend much of practice preparing for South Carolina's stingy zone defense. "Good outside shooting and penetration," Phelps reminds the team. "That's the only way to beat them."

* * *

I'm sure South Carolina will be very emotional after Buck Freeman's unfortunate death yesterday. Buck coached Frank McGuire at St. John's and had been Frank's assistant for many years. McGuire himself has been sick lately, though I wouldn't be surprised to see him back on the bench tomorrow. His return after a five-game absence would give South Carolina a big psychological boost.

## SATURDAY, FEBRUARY 16

The dapper Gamecock coach has, indeed, rejoined his team for today's regionally televised game, but Notre Dame discovers unexpected incentive of its own. Encouraged by Oregon State's stunning 61–57 upset of UCLA last night, Digger exults in the dressing room, "You can be number one again if you win today. Now go out there and do it."

The early play of both teams is more desultory than inspired, since the Irish man-to-man and the Gamecock zone are barely penetrable. Ten shots and more than four minutes separate Notre Dame's first and second baskets, but they are sufficient to tie the score 4–4.

The Irish improve their marksmanship later on to take a 31–26 half-time lead. After seven minutes of the second period they have an eleven-point advantage, which forces South Carolina out of its zone. The Gamecocks allow only four more field goals, but Notre Dame capitalizes on nineteen of twenty-four free-throw opportunities—ten after Phelps orders the four corners with 4:45 left and the score 62–54.

South Carolina manages to cut the margin to four points at 1:34, but its hopes die when star guard Brian Winters misses two free throws and commits his fourth and fifth fouls. The Irish win 72–68 as Dantley sets a school record with an eleven-for-eleven foul-shooting display. Brokaw does not shoot well, but his game-high fifteen rebounds represent a career best.

The team is in fine spirits during the return trip to South Bend. With another streak broken, their twenty-first win secured, and UCLA defeated, there is hopeful talk of being number one again. What the Irish don't yet know is that the Bruins have lost still another game, a 56–51 upset to Oregon. Such unexpected circumstances naturally lend themselves to an impromptu pep rally—and that's exactly what happens when the team is greeted on campus about 9:00 P.M. by 1,000 students. Phelps even lets some of the freshmen say a few words.

Later in the evening, the enthusiasm spills over to a local theater. When Shumate, Brokaw, and Clay walk in to see *The Exorcist,* they receive a standing ovation.

\* \* \*

The national picture has changed a lot in the last two days. South Carolina is one of our best wins of the year, but it's overshadowed by UCLA's losses. I'm very happy for Dick Harter and his Oregon team. I know Dick felt the same way when we beat UCLA.

The Bruins haven't lost two straight games since the 1966 season, the only year in the last ten they didn't win the national championship. Their losses certainly weren't predictable. My only guess is that Wooden's having a personality problem with some of his players. He's very set in his ways, and there are several free-thinkers on the team. It could be a situation that's been brewing for a long time without anyone's realizing it.

I definitely think we should be number one now. Our road schedule is tougher than North Carolina State's, and we've beaten five current Top 20 teams, while they have defeated only two. We did lose to UCLA by nineteen points, but that was on their floor after we had already beaten them. State played the Bruins on a neutral court and lost by eighteen, with Walton missing half the game. I really don't think there is any question about who should be number one.

## SUNDAY, FEBRUARY 17

Notre Dame does not look like a number-one contender in today's practice. The road trip that made it the first Irish team in history to post twenty wins in so few games has left the players tired and dragging.

In fact, the same might be said of their performance over the second half of the season. Notre Dame has won all eight games since the UCLA loss, but by only half its previous point margin. The main reason for the decline has been its play in the second half of those games. The Irish have been outscored five times in the final twenty minutes, and only once—against DePaul—were they more dominant in the second half than in the first.

Nevertheless, Notre Dame is winning, and that's all the players and coaches really care about. Western Michigan, coming in tomorrow with a 12–9 record, should be no great problem.

\* \* \*

Considering that four of our last five games were on the road, I'm very pleased with our situation right now. With only five games left, and four of those at home, I'm starting to think more and more about the regionals. I think Notre Dame and Marquette are certain for the Mideast, with Indiana probably representing the Big Ten, and either Vanderbilt or Alabama the Southeastern

Conference. I hope it's Vanderbilt, because I would hate to play Alabama on its home court in Tuscaloosa, especially after what happened in the Sugar Bowl.

## MONDAY, FEBRUARY 18

Phelps starts Martin at point guard against Western Michigan and tells Clay he will not play unless he's needed.

He's needed all right—sprained ankle and all.

Brokaw is on the bench with three quick fouls and Notre Dame is trailing 21–16, when Digger hustles the little guard into the fray. Dwight doesn't score in eight minutes of duty, but he guides the Irish to a 33–33 tie, and the half ends at thirty-seven apiece.

The game remains close deep into the second half, when Notre Dame finally steadies its ball-handling, oils its fast break, and plugs its defensive gaps. Brokaw and Dantley contribute seven points each to a seven-minute, 21–4 spurt which makes the score 71–52. The Irish go on to win 85–68, permitting only one Bronco to reach double figures.

\* \* \*

This is the third straight season Western Michigan has given us a tough game here. But as I told the team afterwards, everyone is psyched for us because we're having such a great year. I'm sure it will be the same in our remaining home games, even though West Virginia, Ball State, and Villanova don't have outstanding records.

I wanted to give Clay a chance to rest his ankle, but he came through to give us a lift when we needed it. Dwight and everyone else will be taking the next two days off before we start preparing for West Virginia on Thursday.

## TUESDAY, FEBRUARY 19

Notre Dame has fallen short in its bid to regain national leadership. Both wire-service polls place N.C. State on top, followed by the Irish and UCLA. The Associated Press voting gives the Wolfpack thirty first-place ballots for 1,034 points and Notre Dame twenty-two for 1,018. Three die-hards have stayed with UCLA, and one voter favored once-beaten Vanderbilt.

\* \* \*

I'm disappointed we weren't voted number one, but this should give us that much more incentive for the tournament.

I spent only half a day in the office, so Terry and I could drive to Chicago and see *To Be Young, Gifted, and Black*. We both enjoyed the opportunity to get away.

## WEDNESDAY, FEBRUARY 20

The coaches decide in their morning meeting that tomorrow's practice should emphasize offensive and defensive fundamentals.

"We'll give them the West Virginia game plan on Friday," Phelps says. "I want tomorrow to be like a preseason practice. That way, they can sharpen their execution and review some of our basic offensive and defensive principles."

McLaughlin, who would like to see fundamentals emphasized more anyway, is especially agreeable to this.

The coaches then discuss possible regional opponents. "Let's start scouting some of the people we might run into later on," Phelps says. "I don't know much about those SEC and Ohio Valley teams, and we need to be better prepared for a Mid-American opponent. Western Michigan proved that on Monday night."

\* \* \*

I spent three hours in Washington Hall tonight, listening to a lecture on the Kennedy assassination. If everything the speaker said is true, it seems possible that Oswald was part of a conspiracy. As he explained it, the government is keeping some important evidence locked away until the year 2039. He wants to petition an earlier release, and I think it's a good idea.

Because the assassination occurred back when I was in college, I was amazed to see so many present-day students interested in it.

It's unfortunate that they don't have a John Kennedy to look up to, the way I did. I really liked what he and Bobby stood for—the youthful vigor and high ideals. I'm no longer a kid, but I feel much the same way about Ted Kennedy.

## THURSDAY, FEBRUARY 21

The Notre Dame team poses for its official photograph today, though without Tom Hansen, who is busy elsewhere. Standing at centercourt with their arms obediently behind their backs are seven players, three coaches, one trainer, and one manager. Sitting in front with their hands obediently stretched to their knees are nine players. Sitting with his hands casually folded in his lap is one player, Bill Paterno.

After the players change into their practice uniforms, Phelps tells them that "everything we do from now on, either in practice or in games, will prepare us for the NCAA tournament. I want to eliminate any mistakes that could hurt us."

\* \* \*

The players know the bid is sewn up, so keeping them motivated may be difficult. I don't want them to go flat with that first tournament game just over two weeks away. Then, it's do or die; hopefully, we are going to do.

## FRIDAY, FEBRUARY 22

The Irish spend twenty minutes of today's hour-and-a-half workout scrimmaging. This is unusual on the day before a game, but it is in keeping with Phelps' long-range plans for the tournament.

The rest of the session is pointed toward tomorrow's game with West Virginia. It has been a frustrating season for the Mountaineers, whose one grand moment occurred in an opening-game defeat of Pittsburgh. Although the seventh-ranked Panthers haven't lost since, West Virginia is now 9–13, seven of the losses and seven of the wins having been decided by five points or less.

*   *   *

During lunch today with the visiting Kennedy lecturer I tried as hard to discuss the assassination as he did to talk about basketball. As it turned out, neither of us had much success escaping into the other person's world. This sort of thing happens to me quite often. I met a doctor affiliated with HEW on a recent airplane flight, and while I asked him about cancer research, he asked me about UCLA. No one likes to be wrapped up in his job twenty-four hours a day.

## SATURDAY, FEBRUARY 23

Basketball players live for days when they are quick and strong, when they can run faster and jump higher than any man around, when the ball is a brown leather homing device and the basket a wide-open target.

For Adrian Dantley, this is one of those days.

In the first half-minute against West Virginia, he swishes a twenty-footer, intercepts the inbound pass, and sticks in a lay-up. Two minutes later, he cans a twenty-two-footer. Twenty-six seconds go by and he grabs a rebound, lays the ball back up, and adds a free throw.

The game is not five minutes old when Dantley follows another rebound with his eleventh point. Another steal, another

》 201 《

lay-up. A sharp pass from Novak and a three-point play. Adrian has sixteen points and Notre Dame is leading 34–17 when Paterno replaces him at 10:04.

A minute and a half later, Dantley is back in the game working his way inside, taking a pass from Brokaw, and scoring again. It is now Notre Dame 43—Dantley 18—West Virginia 17.

Another pass from Brokaw, another basket. A foul followed by two free throws. Then Novak replaces him, and he spends the last four minutes, eighteen seconds on the bench. He has twenty-two points, and Notre Dame's half-time lead is 56–36.

Dantley continues his rampage in the first three and a half minutes of the second period. Three baskets inside, and a short-range jumper outside. Seven minutes without a point, then eight points in two minutes. Adrian is hitting jump shots and drives, lay-ups and stick-backs, fall-aways and—yes—one while falling down.

Dantley puts the Irish ahead 93–61 with 6:29 to play, and less than a minute later, Crotty replaces him. As Adrian walks to the bench, the capacity crowd salutes his forty-one-point performance with a standing ovation. Eighteen field goals in twenty-three attempts, five-for-five from the foul line, twelve rebounds, three steals, two assists, and only one turnover. All in twenty-nine minutes.

When Notre Dame's 108–80 victory is complete, Dantley says, "I had forty-four points in a high school game once, but this is a bigger thrill. I was hoping to have a good game because I haven't played well in some of the others on television."

And how soon did he know he had it?

"When I scored my second basket after stealing that pass. I felt good then, real good."

Adrian played a tremendous game today. He was hitting his shots and filling the lane on the fast break. When a player is doing all that—and he's got someone like Brokaw handing out ten assists—he has to have a great game.

Actually, we needed a good performance by Adrian, because the other players were off in their shooting. Dwight went oh-for-five and he seemed very discouraged when he came out. He just can't shake that ankle injury; it really has him down.

I was very pleased with our defensive play, which caused twenty-two turnovers. The extra time we spent on fundamentals definitely improved the rotation and double-teaming in our presses.

Terry and I went out tonight with Ara and Katie, and some people involved with a celebrity golf tournament in Dayton which will benefit multiple sclerosis. After dinner, we all went over to the Parseghians' house and listened to Ara play the organ.

## SUNDAY, FEBRUARY 24

Notre Dame is 22–1 and ranked second in the country, and Shumate is contemplating the reasons why. "Talent more than anything," he decides on this off day. "We have a lot of good players, and nobody's jealous of the other guy. You never see anyone begging for the ball in a game, because we're one coherent unit. Digger helps by treating everyone the same. He's fair, so there's no dissension. I won't say I don't get mad at him sometimes. He can get so hostile in practice that I hate him. But that only makes me play harder in a game. Afterwards, I'm glad it happened that way."

*　　*　　*

Terry and I experienced some real country living today with some friends who live in Bremen. We ate rabbit, quail, and chicken, quite a change for a steak-and-potatoes man like me. I really enjoyed it.

## MONDAY, FEBRUARY 25

Toby Knight and Ken Wolbeck are going at each other in practice while Shumate agitates from the sideline. "C'mon, Tobe," he mocks. "Get physical in there."

The aggressive play by the splintery freshman and the raw-boned senior intensifies when they collide while chasing a loose ball. Wolbeck winds up in the bleachers, and as he returns to the court, he clenches his fists. The freshman is showing him up and he doesn't like it.

In fact, it's irritated Ken all season that he, Stevens, and Schmelzer aren't on the traveling squad. "It's a bad deal," he said recently. "Of course, we're not good enough to play regularly, but we should get to make the trips. We know the game better than the freshmen who just sit on the bench. We're seniors and we've put in our time, but we aren't getting any reward."

Later in the scrimmage, Wolbeck sends Bill Drew sprawling as he fights through a screen which has separated him from

Knight. While Drew writhes on the floor with an injured leg, Wolbeck growls to Knight, "You're next, Toby."

Practice concludes without any more flareups.

\* \* \*

Although Ball State's 14–10 record isn't bad, I'm hoping we can take a big early lead against them tomorrow. The reserves have worked hard in practice all season, and they deserve more playing time than I've given them.

## TUESDAY, FEBRUARY 26

The Cardinals are tougher than expected. They go ahead 12–10 after six minutes, largely on four baskets by Larry Bullington, the nation's sixth-leading scorer. On this evening, however, Shumate, the nation's eighteenth-leading scorer, is more productive. Notre Dame pulls away to a 50–38 half-time advantage, with Shumate outscoring Bullington 19–14.

Brokaw tightens his defense against the Ball State star in the second half, and the 26-point-per-game scorer can add only one more basket. Shumate, meanwhile, continues to overpower the Cardinals under the basket and finishes with thirty-one points, equaling his career high set last year against St. John's. Shumate also chalks up fifteen rebounds and five assists in the 93–69 victory.

Despite the margin of Notre Dame's twentieth consecutive home win, no reserve sees more than three minutes of action. Phelps says later that he did not feel comfortable until the team spurted from seventeen to twenty-eight points ahead with two minutes left.

Ball State kept us from going to the bench early by staying within striking distance right until the end. I just hope the reserves weren't too disappointed. They can still be a part of a national championship team by working hard and making contributions in practice. It's a once-in-a-lifetime opportunity which can be realized only if everyone accepts his role.

## WEDNESDAY, FEBRUARY 27

Another day off for the players; for the coaches, another day to think about the tournament.

"There's one thing in particular we have to improve," Phelps says in the morning meeting. "We're not getting back on defense fast enough after scoring. The other teams are breaking right past us because we're not hustling, and our heads are turned the wrong way. It's one of our major weaknesses, and it could cost in the tournament. Let's not beat ourselves the way we did against Virginia Tech last year."

"I know what you mean," says DiBiaso. "Clay didn't box out, and his man picked up the loose ball and scored the winning basket."

The analysis inspires some new posters for McLaughlin to hang in the dressing room. One will read:

> The Only Way We
> Will Get Beat
> Is If We Beat
> OURSELVES

The other:

NIT—Box Out

NCAA—Getting Back

Tonight, Phelps reviews the last reel of the Indiana game film. The Hoosiers have almost wrapped up the Big Ten title, and the tournament showdown, which seemed possible in December, appears probable now.

*　*　*

All of our hard work will be rewarded tomorrow when the bids come out. I'm sure the tournament committee will put us in the Mideast region, though I hate the idea of having to play in Tuscaloosa. No matter whom we go against down there, the crowd will really be on us. If it's Alabama, we won't have a chance.

## THURSDAY, FEBRUARY 28

Notre Dame's invitation to the NCAA tournament comes in a morning telephone call to Moose Krause. As one of nine at-large teams in a field of twenty-five, the Irish will play their first-round game in Terre Haute, Indiana, on March 9 against Ohio Valley champion Austin Peay. The winner will advance to the Mideast Regional in Tuscaloosa, to face the Big Ten representative on March 14.

Only two other schools (UCLA and Kentucky) have made more appearances in the thirty-six-year-old tournament than Notre Dame. But once entered, the Irish have compiled an undistinguished record. In ten previous trips, Notre Dame has gotten as far as the regional finals only three times. On four occasions, they went home after their first game. The school's overall record in the NCAA tournament is 10–12.

In anticipation of today's announcement, Phelps has prepared a memorandum which he now discusses with DiBiaso and McLaughlin. Entitled "Preparation for NCAA–1974," it outlines the responsibilities of players and coaches during the tournament period, "through the final game on March 25th."

The duties of the assistants break down this way: DiBiaso will be in charge of scouting; McLaughlin tickets, game films, and "locker room signs and gimmicks." Both will share responsibility for "team control" on the road—"bed checks, floor policing, plugging phones"—and both are to assist in game preparation and strategy. Phelps emphasizes that "all office administration must be geared to the NCAA tournament. Till March 25, everything else is secondary." Except for "phone calls to prospects," recruiting activities will be curtailed "until the NCAA tournament is over."

Phelps has two major duties: game preparation and strategy, and public relations and press interviews.

Finally, he lists the players' responsibilities: "Accept your role during the NCAA tournament . . . handle all public relations with the help of Roger Valdiserri's office . . . sign autographs . . . be willing to sacrifice points and playing time . . . be responsible in your training habits (diet and rest) . . . be aware of your appearance at all times—till March 25 . . . develop the attitude needed to win the National Championship . . . be willing to work hard and concentrate for three weeks . . . keep in touch with DeCicco on your academic standing."

This is Phelps' battle plan. With it, he hopes to bleach the stains left by last year's NIT defeat, and Fordham's loss to Villanova in the first game of the 1971 Eastern Regionals. "Five wins—National Champions!!" the memo enthuses. That's all there is to it.

Austin Peay upset Jacksonville in the first round of last year's tournament. I don't know much about them, except that Fly Williams has been one of the top scorers in the country for the last two seasons. Frank will scout them on Saturday and meet us before the Dayton game on Monday. Dick will scout Indiana's game against Ohio State Saturday.

It's pleasing to see that we have beaten two of the nine teams which were invited today: South Carolina and Marquette. I expected them to be asked, but I'm a little surprised about Dayton. Their invitation will only make them tougher on Monday. With both of us headed for the tournament, it should be quite a game.

Incidentally, I was pleasantly surprised to read Adrian's opinion of the freshman rule in today's *Observer*. He told the writer, Greg Corgan, that he opposes first-year eligibility, just as I do. Adrian added, of course, that he would never have come here if we didn't let freshmen play.

## FRIDAY, MARCH 1

February was a bad month for Dwight Clay. Not that it started out that way. His girl friend was at the Davidson game to see him score nineteen points, two fewer than his career high. He put in twelve more against Michigan State, giving him consecutive games in double figures for the first time since early December.

But it was pure frustration after that. Twelve points in the last seven games, five baskets in thirty-two attempts. That's not the Iceman. That's embarrassing. Every kid in the Pittsburgh hill section can do better than that.

And all because of an ankle injury. It just won't go away.

When Phelps tells Clay he wants to rest him against Villanova tomorrow and possibly against Dayton on Monday, Dwight objects. "I've got to play," he says. "I've got to get my game back together. It won't get better if I sit on the bench."

Digger is sympathetic, but unyielding. "The more you play, the more you aggravate your injury, Dwight. You have to be a hundred percent for the tournament, not ninety or ninety-five."

Reluctantly, Clay agrees.

\* \* \*

Dwight needs the rest, and Martin can use the experience of playing in his place. Besides, with Dick and Frank scouting tomorrow, I'll need an assistant coach. Dwight is supposed to be our coach on the floor; now he can try being one on the bench.

We're planning to give special recognition to the seniors tomorrow, since it's their last home game. Stevens, Schmelzer, Wolbeck, and Hansen have played very little this year, and I want them in there together along with junior Tom Varga. The Notre Dame program has come a long way in their three varsity seasons, and I'm very grateful for their contributions. They're as much a part of this year's success as anyone.

## SATURDAY, MARCH 2

Notre Dame's basketball fortunes looked bleak two years ago, and the signs were visible everywhere. One literally hung in the Huddle Snack Bar, posted by a discouraged fan wanting to sell his season ticket. A scribbled reply at the bottom showed more optimism, however. "You'll be sorry," it read, "when the Goose is an All-American."

Season tickets aren't so loosely offered these days, but All-Americans don't come in six-point, six-rebound-a-game packages either. Nevertheless, Novak and the four other seniors are due the special recognition given before today's game against Villanova. The ceremony includes an appropriate presentation to Gary: a genuine honker.

After the feathered goose has been carried away, the hairy Goose scores ten points and corrals seven rebounds, and the Irish rip the Wildcats 115–85. Five other players score in double figures for the team's biggest offensive show of the year. Afterwards, Villanova coach Roland Massimino praises, "They're as good as anybody we've faced—and that includes North Carolina State."

Somewhat less menacing were the four Irish seniors and one junior who played the last 3:07 of the game. After Phelps sent them in with Notre Dame ahead 103–76, they outscored the Wildcats 12–9. Stevens and Varga tallied two of the baskets, and Wolbeck and Schmelzer had one each.

With this modest showing, the careers of the four senior reserves come to an end. Stevens, however, will continue playing after graduation in Belgium. Schmelzer and Hansen hope to coach, while Wolbeck will join the Caterpillar Tractor Company in Peoria.

Of the four, Stevens is most disappointed about his limited college-playing experience. "I came off the bench to help us beat Kansas in overtime last year," he remembers, "but Digger never used me in a clutch situation again. That soured my whole attitude."

Despite the disappointment of not making the traveling squad, Wolbeck says, "I stuck it out because I love Notre Dame. I'd even like to help recruit players in my area, because there's not a better place to go to school."

Schmelzer assesses his experiences with more equanimity. "I'm satisfied," he says. "I'll never have more freedom and less responsibility again. It really didn't bother me so much that I didn't play or travel. I just wanted to be part of the team. I realized in my sophomore year that there was something worthwhile about studying, so I concentrated on that."

And how, finally, do they view their coach?

"Both of us have outgoing personalities," says Stevens. "I think we were both vying for the limelight, and we didn't get along because of it."

"I don't like the way Digger yells at the players," says Wolbeck. "There's no need to talk to a twenty-one-year-old the way he does. We can be reasoned with. But I can't complain about the results. He's a good coach and I respect him, even if I don't agree with his style."

Schmelzer believes Phelps' acerbic temper indicates that "he hasn't matured yet as a coach. He's awfully critical of the players sometimes. I learned in class that to get the best out of someone, you shouldn't make him feel like a failure." Schmelzer notes, however, that his biggest complaint does not relate to Phelps at all. "It's Shumate," he says. "When we're in the dressing room, he always plays the music he wants to hear. Nobody else matters."

\* \* \*

We had an all-around good effort against Villanova today. Ray Martin did especially well, but Dwight will be back in the lineup Monday.

A final word on the seniors. They are the only ones

who can fully appreciate our progress since that 6–20 season. They may have been behind the scenes, but they were the backbone of the squad. When they look back someday and see what they helped build, they will be very proud.

The Big Ten race opened up today when Indiana was upset 85–79 at Ohio State. As I said in December, the Buckeyes are tough at home.

## SUNDAY, MARCH 3

McLaughlin and DiBiaso are already in Dayton when the team arrives by bus. While Frank saw Austin Peay lose 74–71 yesterday to Murray State, Dick watched Ohio State upset Indiana in Columbus and then hurried to Dayton to catch the Flyers' victory last night over Northern Michigan. Dayton is now 18–7 overall, losing only to Louisville in fifteen home games.

Shumate is irked today because of an encounter he had at a law students' party last night. "Some guy started giving me all that talk about being my agent. There I was trying to have a good time and he was taking advantage of me. Every time somebody starts getting nice and friendly, I know they will eventually get around to that."

\*   \*   \*

We'll start out in our zone defense for the first time tomorrow night. We zoned Dayton last year and won 94–58, our biggest margin of the season. I've thought all along that this could be a tough game. I just hope the players are ready for it. It would be nice to take a 25–1 record into the tournament.

## MONDAY, MARCH 4

Phelps has some kind words for Dayton coach Don Donoher in a speech to the luncheon meeting of the Agonis Club today. Digger praises his colleague's record and chastises those who supported the "Dump Donoher" movement when the Flyer program was sagging. Back at the motel, Digger elaborates: "Fans just don't understand what coaches and their families go through. There are up cycles and down cycles, and everyone should accept that. We're just as sensitive as anyone else."

Notre Dame's defensive strategy—a 1-2-2 zone—suits the hot-shooting Flyers perfectly. With guards Donald Smith and Johnny Davis hitting one jump shot after another, Dayton goes ahead in the second minute of play and zooms to a fifteen-point advantage, with 5:31 remaining. A late Irish rally makes the half-time score 44–38. In a devastating display of long-range accuracy, Dayton has canned fourteen shots from outside—six by Smith and four by Davis—and gone twenty-two for thirty-eight overall. Notre Dame is fifteen for thirty-five, but its real problem is a listlessness which Phelps' dressing-room fervor can't penetrate.

The Irish stay within four points of Dayton through half of the second period before falling behind by eleven. They struggle to within seven at 4:50 on two free throws by Dantley and a steal and lay-up by Shumate. A minute later, however, Adrian commits his fourth foul, the raging Phelps picks up a technical, and Smith sinks three straight free throws and his twelfth jumper of the night.

The Irish do not threaten again. In the last minutes of Dayton's 97–82 upset victory, a record home crowd of 13,528 serenades, "Goodbye, Irish. We hate to see you go."

While Smith was scoring thirty-two points and Dayton was making 58 percent of its shots, Notre Dame stumbled along with 41 percent. The dependable Shumate played brilliantly, with twenty-nine points, sixteen rebounds, and three steals, but the other four starters combined to hit only fourteen of forty-seven shots.

"We just couldn't get up for this game," Dantley whispers as the players shower quietly.

Meanwhile, in the Dayton dressing room there is only rejoicing. Coach Donoher gloats, "This is the greatest win we've had since I've been here."

* * *

Well, it was a long time between losses, but I've got to give Dayton a lot of credit. Smith is a great shooter, and the Flyers played very, very well. It didn't slow them down at all when three players picked up three fouls in the first half.

As for ourselves, we didn't execute offensively or defensively, and we lacked our usual intensity. No one helped Shumate or Dantley on the boards, and we missed a lot of easy shots.

I guess it's ironic that we lost, because earlier in the season I thought a defeat just before the tournament might be good. But I certainly didn't feel that way during the game. All I could think about was coming back to win. As for the tournament, I don't see how this game will help us at all. We just didn't play well.

## TUESDAY, MARCH 5

Phelps is in his office fretting over the Dayton loss when Roger Valdiserri comes in with some good news. The sports information director tells Digger that both United Press International and *The Sporting News* have named him Coach of the Year. His margin over Wooden in the UPI vote was a healthy 107 to 43.

Phelps does not find some other news so pleasant, however. A letter to the editor and an accompanying editorial in the *Observer* demands that the nontraveling seniors be taken with the rest of the team to Greensboro.

Though the letter was not signed by his seniors, Digger believes they were responsible. He orders Schmelzer to his office immediately. When Greg arrives, Phelps makes two points vividly clear. The team has to win three more games before anyone goes to Greensboro. And then, if the opportunity does arise, he intends—as he has all year—that everyone make the trip. "Why didn't you trust me?" he asks. "Why make such an issue of a team matter?"

\* \* \*

I am very pleased and proud to have been honored with those Coach of the Year awards today. I honestly believe I owe my selection to Dick, Frank, and the eighteen players. But I must admit that I am much too concerned about the Austin Peay game to enjoy it completely. When the tournament is over, I'll feel differently.

## WEDNESDAY, MARCH 6

There is a brief letter to the editor in the *Observer* today referring to a "misunderstanding" of circumstances on the basketball team which "resulted in rumors blown entirely out of proportion." In short, "there is no problem." The letter is signed by Greg Schmelzer, Chris Stevens, and Ken Wolbeck.

An item in today's papers announces betting odds for all possible tournament participants. Although UCLA must still defeat USC to assure the Pacific-8 title, the Bruins are a 2–1 favorite. North Carolina State, which must win the ACC tournament before it can participate, is the 3–1 choice. Notre Dame is third at 4–1. North Carolina and Maryland follow with 7–1 and 8–1 odds. Listed at 200–1 is the still undetermined (or unknown) "Big Sky champion."

*　*　*

We took yesterday off and began to prepare for Austin Peay today. Based on Frank's scouting report, they could be tough. They have great quickness and a halfcourt zone press which really bothered Kentucky in the regionals last year. Of course, they have Fly Williams too. We're not expecting Novak to stop him completely, but we do hope Gary's two-inch height advantage can throw his shooting off a little. Dwight can also help by making it difficult for the point guard to pass Fly the ball.

Our biggest advantage should be our superior front-court size. But that won't mean very much if Fly gets hot, and they start fast-breaking up- and downcourt. I don't want our players to be lulled by the Governors' 17–9 record, either. Seven of those defeats were by four points or less.

## THURSDAY, MARCH 7

Monday's loss to Dayton has not shaken the players' confidence. "I think it helped us," says Brokaw while toweling off after practice. "It made us realize that things don't always come easy. Besides, the tournament is a new season, just like the pro playoffs."

Clay's easy mobility indicates that his ankle may finally be strong again. "I'm ready now," he says. "It doesn't hurt any more and I'm not worrying about it either."

\* \* \*

I summed up my feelings on the tournament today by telling a reporter to forget the rankings, forget the odds, and forget the favorites. There's going to be plenty of upsets before the four regional winners are decided, and there could even be one or two surprises in Greensboro. It's always been that way in the past—at least until the final game, which UCLA has always won.

## FRIDAY, MARCH 8

Notre Dame arrives in Terre Haute with a thick dossier of accomplishments. The Irish stand second in the polls, second in field-goal percentage (.530), third in won-lost percentage (.923), eighth in both scoring (88.9) and winning margin (16.4), and tenth in rebound margin (9.7). By comparison, top-ranked N.C. State places among the top ten in four statistical categories.

Only the 1909 Irish team, which finished 33–7, won more games. Only the 19–1 clubs of 1926 and 1927 had higher winning percentages (.950). The 1974 team's lofty rank in the polls, and Phelps' multiple Coach of the Year awards are both unprecedented. But can the best Irish team in history end the school's long tournament famine?

Gleaming, new Hulman Center on Indiana State's campus bustles this afternoon, as the four teams in tomorrow's double-header go through hour-long workouts and an NBC television crew prepares for tomorrow's coverage. While the Irish wait to practice, Digger tells the players, "It's going to take dedication and concentration to beat Austin Peay. This could be our biggest game of the tournament. We know all the other teams we might play—Indiana, Marquette, Kansas, UCLA. We've beaten them once; now let's beat Austin Peay."

After a brisk workout, Marquette takes the floor to prepare for Mid-American champion Ohio University. As the Warriors go through their drills, Al McGuire strolls over to Phelps. "That Dayton loss will help you," McQuire says. "I think it was good for you."

"I hope so, Al," Phelps sighs, "but I'm not sure."

"Maybe I'm wrong," McGuire continues, "but that's what I think."

"I just hope both of us get to Alabama."

The Irish are also very much on the mind of Austin Peay coach Lake Kelly. "They are big and strong," he says. "We can't let Shumate and Dantley destroy us inside. But I think we match up well with Brokaw and Clay. I'm not worried as much about those two." Asked about twenty-eight-point-per-game sophomore Fly Williams, Kelly adds, "This is a special game for him. He could really turn on for national television."

This evening Terre Haute gussies itself up to welcome the visiting schools with a banquet. The fruit cups are still chilled when Shumate notices that the Austin Peay and Ohio players came casually dressed and Marquette's didn't come at all. "Just look at us," he grumbles, fiddling with his tie. "There's too much regimentation on this team. City players aren't used to that."

\* \* \*

We're in good physical condition for the first time in a month. I hope our mental outlook is sound too, because I'm not sure everyone is taking Austin Peay seriously enough.

We're so close to fulfilling all of our dreams that I would hate to see anything go wrong. One win gets us to Alabama, two more take us to Greensboro. Reaching the final four is the ambition of every coach in the country. You may not win the championship, but you can't lose the distinction of having been there. That's something I've always wanted.

## SATURDAY, MARCH 9

If the 10,100 spectators in Hulman Center want tense, competitive basketball today, they came to the wrong arena. Marquette's 85–59 victory over Ohio is a breeze compared to the hurricane Notre Dame unleashes against Austin Peay.

After playing even for the first three minutes, the Irish string together thirteen straight points to lead 19–6. Brokaw scores six, all on snappy passes from Clay, who cans an eighteen-foot jump-shot of his own. Fly Williams, the one-man firing squad, twice brings the Governors within six before Notre Dame can break away to a comfortable 54–34 half-time lead.

"You did a helluva job," Phelps exults in the dressing room. "Just don't let them come back."

The Irish aren't about to. The finely tuned team wins 108–66 by forcing twenty-two turnovers, handing out thirty assists (nine by Clay), outshooting the Governors 60 percent to 36, and out-rebounding them 51–37. Brokaw, at his magical best, tallies twenty-five points.

Super Fly, meanwhile, has to shoot thirty-one times to score a game-high twenty-six points. His five rebounds are half his average, and he is hounded into six turnovers. In short, Novak does a very creditable defensive job.

"We've never played a better team," says Lake Kelly as his Governors pack to go home. "They fill every position with just the right kind of player. When they are like this, the only team with a chance of beating them is UCLA."

And why not? Notre Dame's forty-two-point margin is more than just an Irish postseason record; it is the sixth-highest spread in NCAA tournament history.

\* \* \*

It's hard to believe the team which beat Austin Peay today is the same one which lost to Dayton on Monday. We were as intense and aggressive this afternoon as we were flat the other night. We did everything well.

I was particularly pleased with Shumate's unselfishness. He took a pounding in the first half without losing his temper or trying to force his own scoring opportunities. He simply gave up the ball and let somebody else shoot. John hasn't had a poor game all year. He deserves every bit of the All-American recognition he receives.

Now it's on to Tuscaloosa. We're only two wins from Greensboro and four from a national championship.

Notre Dame's first Mideast Regional opponent will be the winner of the Big Ten playoff between Indiana and Michigan tomorrow night in Champaign, Illinois. To Phelps, this could only mean the Hoosiers.

"Except for the loss to Ohio State, they've improved since we beat them," DiBiaso says in a late-afternoon meeting.

"I think we're better off spending the next two days on Indiana anyway," Phelps says. "If Michigan wins, we could have some match-up problems, but Indiana would be tougher overall. Indiana does more than Michigan, and if we're ready for Indiana, we're ready for Michigan too."

Later in the evening, players and coaches spend an hour and a half reviewing the well-worn Indiana film. "We want to attack Indiana a little differently this time," Phelps announces, "and make some defensive adjustments too. We'll go over everything in practice tomorrow."

\* \* \*

According to the morning paper, my prediction about upsets almost came true last night. N.C. State had to go into overtime to beat Maryland in the ACC finals, 103–100. It would've been quite a surprise to see the top-ranked team beaten. With the East Regionals and national finals being played in North Carolina, they have a chance to go a long way.

As for UCLA, I watched them beat Southern California, 82–52, on television. I couldn't believe the 46–13 half-time score. Judging by their intensity, the Bruins are back. It was a surprise, however, to see them in a 2-3 offense with Tommy Curtis and Greg Lee in the backcourt. Now that they're going with two guards, Marques Johnson—who played so well against us—is back on the bench. Apparently, Wooden had to change his offense to keep peace in the family. If we play them again, I'll have to give that new offense a lot of thought.

## MONDAY, MARCH 11

Novak receives a letter of acceptance from Loyola of Chicago today, ending his year-long uncertainty about medical school.

"I'm still waiting to hear from three or four others," Gary says at lunch, "but it feels good to have one confirmed."

Now his only unfulfilled college ambition is the national championship. "I think I'm helping us get there by giving the ball off to the other guys. They want to play pro ball anyway, so maybe it's good that they get more scoring chances. I know how important my goals have been to me, and I want to help them accomplish theirs."

Novak does not miss his twenty-point-per-game sophomore days. "Then, I was getting the ball and I was expected to score. I just contributed what I could. Now, people want to know why I don't score more. They're too concerned with the Waltons and other superstars. Digger bugs me, too, when he tells me I'm not a good shooter. Granted, we didn't win much two years ago, but when we did, I was the one scoring."

As for Phelps' short-fused coaching style, Novak says, "Actually, I think he's been a lot better this year. He used to get even more upset about things, but now he isn't so quick to overreact."

For two and a half hours this afternoon, the prep team simulates Indiana's familiar offense and defense. Tonight,

Digger turns on his television, hoping the Hoosiers will make the preparation worthwhile.

But Michigan wins 75–67.

* * *

Even though we've prepared for Indiana, maybe it's better not to play them again. Beating a good team twice in one season is very difficult. Now we have to change gears and go with Dick's scouting report on Michigan. The Wolverines have defeated us twice in the last two years, but we've revenged old losses all season. We have to do it again.

## TUESDAY, MARCH 12

Because of the Dayton loss, Notre Dame has dropped to third in the polls, behind N.C. State and UCLA. But it's the twelfth-ranked team—Michigan—which interests the coaches.

"I guess we made a mistake in our calculations," McLaughlin says this morning.

"Yeah," sighs Phelps, "I guess we did."

Like the Irish, the Wolverines are young and small. Unlike the Irish, they have less depth, less precision and explosiveness in their fast-break offense, and less resolve in their man-to-man defense.

What Michigan does do, however, is win—ten victories in their last eleven games, twenty-one of twenty-five overall. Even so, the Wolverines are seldom overpowering. Half of their conference triumphs are by four points or less, and their average scoring margin is only eight points. All the losses came on the road—by eleven points to Detroit, twenty to

UCLA, one to Purdue, and twelve to Indiana.

Michigan's one outstanding player in an otherwise unspectacular lineup is Campanella (Campy) Russell. The 6′ 8″ junior forward leads his team in scoring (23.3) and assists (99), and is second in rebounds to burly center C. J. Kupec, (10.7 to 11.9). Russell is the complete offensive player, with quick moves to the basket and a deadly long-range shooting touch. He won or shared team scoring honors in all but four games.

*  *  *

Obviously, our biggest problem against Michigan will be Russell. It's another tough defensive assignment for Goose, but he has to accept the challenge. Kupec is very physical, so we must stop him on the boards as well as slow the Wolverine fast break. We can take advantage of their depth problem by wearing them down with our own fast break and applying constant defensive pressure. If we can only play our game and not beat ourselves, we will win.

## WEDNESDAY, MARCH 13

One last practice for Michigan, and the Irish are on their way by chartered plane to Tuscaloosa.

Much to the players' relief, their attendance is not expected at tonight's pretournament dinner. Shumate goes out with some friends from the Michigan team as well as a few blacks from Alabama's. Thanks to shrewd groundwork laid by Novak at the Sugar Bowl, several of the players have dates lined up. Those who don't, take their chances in forays along sorority row.

At the dinner, each of the four coaches is asked to speak briefly. Michigan's John Orr incessantly bubbles, "We're just so proud to be here," before calming down to admit, "This is the first time I've ever been in an NCAA tournament, so I really don't know how to act."

Al McGuire would like to point out, "before anyone else does," that he has been to five regionals and left as a loser every time. "I'd like to change that," he says, "but I don't know if it really matters. UCLA is going to win it all again anyway."

Phelps gets in a few jibes about the Sugar Bowl—which don't exactly bring down the house—and Vanderbilt coach Roy Skinner apologizes for not being as funny as the other coaches.

When the dinner is over, Phelps says, "Al may be willing to let UCLA have it again, but I'm not."

\* \* \*

I hope the people down here are as friendly tomorrow night as they were today. There sure won't be many fans supporting us. Everybody seems to be saving their money and making plans for Greensboro. I'd like some support in Tuscaloosa first. Because of the spring break, we won't even have our cheerleaders or band here. We tried to get a local high school band, but it was on spring break too.

## THURSDAY, MARCH 14

It seems an unnecessary hardship, since plenty of seats were available on the team charter, but Greg Schmelzer and *Observer* Sports Editor Vic Dorr arrive in Tuscaloosa after an arduous fourteen-and-a-half-hour drive. "I'm a team groupie now," Schmelzer says with a weary smile.

Greg joins the players for breakfast as Shumate is talking about his night prowl with the Wolverines. "Campy and Steve Grote seemed confident, really loose," John says between bites of French toast. "They must think they're going to beat us."

After breakfast, the team goes to Memorial Coliseum, where it finds Michigan in a closed practice. "What could they be doing in a half-hour workout," asks Phelps, "that they don't want anyone to see?"

A few minutes later, Notre Dame takes over the arena floor. When the light workout is over, Phelps sets out to tour the Alabama campus. "There are two things I have to see," he says. "Bear Bryant Hall and the TKE house. Maybe I can get somebody to come out and root for us tonight."

For the next hour, Digger scurries around like a candidate on the stump. There isn't an open door in the athletic dorm that he doesn't go through. A thrust of the hand, a genial "Hi, I'm Digger Phelps of Notre Dame," and hopefully a convert. After the whirlwind inspection is over, Phelps concludes, "This place is nice, but I don't like it. When athletes live among themselves for four years, they miss a lot culturally and socially."

Then, it's on to the TKE house, where Digger is disappointed to learn that the Alabama chapter is not nationally affiliated. "Well, that explains it, then," Phelps exclaims to a bewildered fraternity brother. "Ever since I got here, I've been trying to give you some of the secret stuff, like the handshake, and you didn't know what I was doing."

The pregame feeling in the Irish dressing room suggests neither the ebullient confidence which preceded the UCLA win, nor the pained discomfort which foretold the loss. There is, instead, an uninspired normality. The music plays. The players go about their rituals. Phelps watches it all quietly, sitting with his forearms resting on his knees. He's psyching himself, putting on his game-face.

Finally, he rises to speak. If his players need inspiration, he will give it to them. "All the attention is on our friends in the West and our friends in the East," he begins with mock disgust. "Nobody thinks *you* can win this year. *Michigan* doesn't think you can win tonight. Well, it's really nice to play another Big Ten school that stuck it to us."

He's giving it his best shot. "Just remember, everything is going your way. The pressure is on UCLA and N.C. State. We're going to sneak down to Greensboro by doing our thing game-by-game. After all those hours on the playground, after all that work this year, there's just one week left. Three games before we prove who's number one. It's an opportunity that every kid on the playground would like to have. So don't let it end here tonight. Michigan thinks they can beat you. They've beaten you two years in a row. Now, it's time to beat them."

After Phelps repeats the game plan, the players warm up. When they return, Digger musters every bit of his confidence, and the locker room rings with his final words. "You're better than they are. They don't even belong in the Top 20. Now beat them."

As the boos cascade from every level of the arena, it is obvious that Notre Dame is not the people's choice in Tuscaloosa. It's all that Sugar Bowl resentment Phelps had feared, harmonizing with the inherent dislike any tournament favorite engenders.

Notre Dame's lethargic performance for most of the first half is a delight to those who wish it ill. The Irish score first, but Michigan reels off ten straight points. The teams trade two baskets and Michigan adds eight more. Notre Dame finally scores again but the Wolverines sink three baskets to go up by twenty, 28–8, with 6:29 left. None of Phelps' frantic stratagems, including two time-outs and seven lineup changes, have been effective. Notre Dame is sleepwalking, precariously close to extinction. Michigan isn't playing very well, either—it was ten minutes and six misses before Campy Russell scored his first basket—but the Wolverines are superior to the Irish.

Notre Dame finally comes alive in the next four and a half minutes. Shumate scores nine points—inside, outside, and at the free-throw line—as the Irish go on a more exemplary 17–2 binge. After both teams register four more points, the half ends at 34–29.

Michigan played poorly in the first half—40 percent from the floor, ten turnovers. Notre Dame played worse—33 percent, eleven turnovers. Russell and Shumate were magnificent, however; the Wolverine totaled twelve points and twelve rebounds, Shumate fifteen points and ten rebounds.

The Irish players had expected more from themselves and less from their opponent. But Phelps, relieved that the deficit is a manageable five points, tries to encourage them. "What are you hanging your heads for?" he asks. "Just play your game. You're doing a helluva job. Any other team would have quit when it fell behind by twenty. You played well for six of twenty minutes. Now go out and play all twenty well. Just keep it going. Keep the momentum going."

The Irish fall behind by nine early in the period and trail 50–44 at 12:58 when Russell scores his twelfth straight point. Shumate answers with a twenty-footer for his ninth in a row, and Notre Dame is within four. The domination of the two superb players is briefly interrupted with baskets from Paterno and Wayman Britt. Then Shumate scores twice more —from inside and on a lay-up following a steal at midcourt— to tie the score 52–52 at 10:13. Seventeen seconds later, Shumate feeds Novak for a left-handed lay-up and the Irish are ahead, the twenty-point deficit miraculously erased, the momentum of the game reversed.

But Russell, scoreless the last four minutes, ties the count again from the top of the key. Another lay-up by Novak, and Campy knots it once more from the right side. The game is a seesaw now, and Notre Dame is the first to fall off. Russell returns the lead to the Wolverines, 58–56, at 8:03. It's 64–60 three and a half minutes later when Michigan calls time-out. With a four-point lead and two players carrying four personals, the Wolverines go into a stall. Michigan is sloppy in its execution—missing six of thirteen free throws, and losing not two, but three, starters—but the Irish cannot take advantage. They are, in fact, inept.

The arena swells with anticipation as the Irish stumble along before their final fall. The score soars to 77–66 with thirty-three seconds left, but Phelps will not give up. Dreams do not die easily. His shout is not audible over the tumult, but the words he forms are clearly distinguishable. "YOU CAN STILL WIN THE GAME." But Michigan wins 77–68. Shumate's thirty-four points and seventeen rebounds aren't enough. Russell has thirty-six and eighteen. Dantley's two points are a season low; Brokaw's ten, just one above his. So what if Michigan makes only 43 percent of its shots? Notre Dame can hit but 39 percent.

Phelps' first move when he comes into the hushed dressing room is to the signs over the blackboard. He wordlessly rips down the reminder about "Getting Back" and the warning not to "Beat OURSELVES." The players sit silently, some with their heads down, some watching their coach's melodrama. When Phelps finally begins to talk, he is hard, biting, as if there were one more half to be played and stern words would save the day. Then he mellows and, as he mellows, he becomes philosophic. "This is what life is all about, men. You have dreams and you try to reach them. You don't always manage it."

He stops to open a stick of gum, and then mourns his innermost regret. "Just once in my life, I wanted to reach the final four. And I thought it would be this year."

He notices Novak on the verge of tears. "That's all right, Goose. Go ahead and cry. Who ever said a man couldn't cry?" And then, after sympathy, disdain. "That's what's wrong with this team. It isn't emotional enough."

There's nothing more to say. Digger walks around the room to each of the players, touching one, shaking another's hand, thanking them all for their contributions. Then he leaves. The outside world wants to know what happened. "Public relations and press interviews"—just as his tournament memo outlined.

With Phelps gone, some of the players begin to peel off their soaked uniforms. Schmelzer, "the groupie," walks among them, shaking hands. No one talks. No one knows what to say. Brokaw sits with a towel around his shoulders, looking down, shaking his head. Shumate is on the floor, squeezed into a corner. The tape deck beside him plays soft, anguished soul.

Finally, Dave Kuzmicz says there's one thing he can't understand. "The guards killed me in practice all week, and today they didn't seem to be doing anything."

Dantley tries to explain his listless play. "My legs," he says, "felt like log cabins." Novak says, "It pisses me off. I really thought we could do it this year." As harsh reality begins to replace shock, Martin laments, "Man, you just don't know how good something is till you lose it."

When Phelps returns from the interview room, he puts his personal disappointment aside to console each player individually. "I want you to keep your head up," he tells Dantley. "Don't let it get you down. Hit the books, and we'll get 'em next year."

He goes to Novak, and gives a weak smile. "The happiest

thing that happened this week was your getting into med school. You just work there the way you have here, and you'll do all right. I've never had a kid give the way you have for three years."

After talking to each of them, Digger goes out to see the second game. Marquette wins 69–61. Saturday afternoon, Notre Dame will play Vanderbilt.

* * *

I don't know what it is that makes a team play the way we did tonight. We just didn't have it, we weren't ready. Give Michigan all the credit you want, but we're a better team. We beat ourselves.

After we went ahead in the second half, I thought we would win. But we lost our spark and couldn't get it back. No one took charge or gave us leadership. I might have put Kuzmicz in, but I didn't have the guts to go with an inexperienced player. Maybe if the crowd had been with us, we could have kept it going.

It didn't bother me so much when UCLA beat us. Considering the circumstances, it was understandable. The Dayton loss disappointed me, but when we came back to play so well against Austin Peay, I didn't worry about it any more. I won't be able to get over this one. I suppose it gets down to one thing. Dantley, Brokaw, Clay, and Novak shot thirteen for forty-eight. When we lost to Dayton, they shot fourteen for forty-seven. Against Austin Peay, they were thirty-one for fifty-three. I never have been much for statistics, but I think those speak for themselves.

We've been burned two years in a row. It's frustrating, sad, and disappointing—more so this time because we had so much to gain. Right now, I feel like a jockey whose horse fell down ten yards from the Kentucky

Derby finish-line. That's how close I thought we were to winning everything.

## FRIDAY, MARCH 15

Not a happy day for the Irish basketball team. "The worst day of my life," Phelps says at breakfast. Terry characterizes it differently. "I was going to write a paper on Edgar Allan Poe while I was down here," she says. "Now I'm in the proper mood for it."

Shumate is in the mood to think about his future. He must finally face the decision to remain at Notre Dame one more year, or graduate with his class in May. "I wonder what people would think if I left?" he asks, sitting up in his motel bed. "There are so many considerations. There's my family. More than anything, I want to be able to help them. And there's the team. I've always wanted to win the big one. If I came back next year, we'd have a good chance. And I hate to leave my friends like Brokaw, Clay, and Adrian. I've got to think about this very seriously."

His thoughts inevitably return to last night's game. "The toughest thing about losing is knowing we let so many people down. Digger and the other coaches really worked hard. And there are all the people who supported us this year. You hate to disappoint the ones who count on you."

After the team works out briefly for tomorrow's consolation game, Clay is asked what he thinks Shumate should do.

"If I were John, I'd probably leave," he answers. "No one should expect him to do any more than he has already."

From a coach's point of view, I would hate to see John go. He's a tremendous basketball player and it would be difficult to replace him. But more than anything, I want him to do what is best for himself. Certainly, if he can make a great deal of money, he should take it. I do think he will be worth more next year, especially if we win the national championship, but he may not want to risk injury. John will get his degree no matter when he leaves, so he really can't make a wrong decision. He has to decide what the best one is.

## SATURDAY, MARCH 16

Consolation games are vile, petty things, played for no good reason except to embarrass the loser and frustrate the winner. But better frustration than embarrassment.

There is an underlying theme in Fr. Riehle's pregame Mass today, which encourages the team to end its season victoriously. Before the game, Phelps is more direct. "We're going out there to win," he tells the players firmly. "We're going to play the way we should have played Thursday."

Vanderbilt no doubt has the same intention. But Notre Dame is smooth, polished, and every bit the team which Phelps—and Fr. Riehle—had hoped to see two nights ago. The Irish lead 60–44 at the half and win 118–88, their twenty-sixth victory in twenty-nine games. Shumate continues his recent brilliant pace with thirty points. Dantley and Brokaw return to their pre-Michigan form with twenty-nine and twenty respectively. Novak scores sixteen, and Clay adds eight points and eight assists. Just as the point margin against Austin Peay was a postseason record, so is the point total today.

Phelps congratulates the team afterwards, but the bitter memory of Thursday's defeat lingers. As Michigan and Marquette warm up for the regional championship game, Digger speaks to his team one last time. "You know, and I know, what we really wanted to accomplish this year," he says. "If we come back next year the way we did today, we've still got a shot at it."

A few hours later, after the Warriors have won 72–70 to join North Carolina State, UCLA, and Kansas in the elite final four, the Marquette and Notre Dame teams meet in the Tuscaloosa airport. McGuire spots Phelps in the lobby and comes over to tell him, "It's too bad, Digger. I really mean it. You guys should be going. There's no way our team compares to yours."

"Thanks, Al," Phelps responds. "If there's anything I can do to help you get ready for Kansas, let me know."

As Notre Dame flies back to South Bend, Digger is struck by a cruel irony. "We beat three of the four teams going to Greensboro," he says.

"It's something to be proud of," someone suggests.

"No it's not," Digger answers. "It only makes me feel worse. UCLA will win again."

There are a dozen or so people awaiting the team's plane. The reception is warm, taking an edge off the disappointment. Phelps seems touched by the welcome. In fact, anyone looking closely might see the young coach of the Notre Dame Fighting Irish fighting back tears.

# AFTERWORD

Three days after the season ended, 1,100 people filled the main floor of the Athletic and Convocation Center to honor the coaches and players at their team banquet. Guest speaker Howard Cosell recalled a similar occasion a few years ago, when he spoke to three hundred Irish fans in a downtown civic building.

Phelps, in an indirect plea to Shumate, told the audience, "What's left of these eighteen men, and those who want to be a part of the Notre Dame family, will go after it again next year."

Shumate's decision was not long in coming, however. A week and a half later, he decided to turn pro because "I had to think of my family first." Phoenix, picking fourth, selected him in the first round of the NBA draft. Shumate chose the Suns over the ABA's Virginia Squires, who had selected him as a future in 1973.

After Shumate's decision, he was invited to play in Pizza Hut's senior all-star game in Las Vegas on April 1. Novak had earlier been voted onto the East team, which Phelps coached to victory over the West.

Shumate, it turned out, would not be the only player to leave Notre Dame with a year of eligibility remaining. Brokaw made himself available to the NBA draft as a junior by joining the league's "hardship list." Milwaukee picked him in the first round and, soon after, Gary signed. "Pro ball is what I always wanted," said Brokaw, "and I saw no reason to wait if a good opportunity came along."

While Phelps was losing two outstanding players in the NBA draft, he and Terry were enjoying a three-week vacation in Europe. It marked Terry's first return to England since she had left as a child.

Digger was back in South Bend a week before the first session of the school's summer basketball camp, which ran from June 16 to June 22. A second session took place from July 21 to July 27, and then Digger conducted his own in West Camp, New York, August 4–10 and August 11–17.

A round of speaking engagements and clinics filled out the summer, and on August 28 Phelps was back at school for the start of the fall semester. The coach's world of Digger Phelps had come full circle.

# RECRUITING FILE

Over a four-year period, an athletic grant-in-aid at the University of Notre Dame is worth sixteen thousand dollars. As permitted by the NCAA, it covers room, board, tuition, books, fees, and laundry. The Irish basketball team awarded four scholarships in the spring of 1974—to 6' 10" Dave Batton of Springfield High in suburban Philadelphia, 6' 6" Randy Haefner of McNicholas High in Cincinnati, 6' 1" Jeff Carpenter of Fenwick High in suburban Chicago, and 6' 2" Donald Williams of Mackin High in Washington.

All four were among the top nine prospects Notre Dame emphasized in its recruiting efforts. They would have been gladly received at almost any school in the country. Among Batton's final choices were Kentucky, Villanova, North Carolina State, and Maryland. Haefner's included Oregon and Miami of Ohio; Carpenter's, Indiana and Wisconsin; Williams', Houston and Washington.

Because of the uncertainty surrounding Shumate's future, Phelps decided early in the year that his primary recruiting objective would be a big man. The big man he got was Batton, the "most likely to succeed" graduate in his high school class, and the only son of a Purdue alumnus.

As recorded in files kept by the Irish coaches, here is how the pursuit and capture of high school All-American Dave Batton progressed in his senior year:

August 21, 1973: Skip Werley, Batton's coach at Springfield High School, writes to Phelps: "This is to confirm that Dave Batton will visit your campus on the weekend of October 27.

. . . Dave has narrowed his choices to 26, rejecting over 150 inquiries, and . . . Notre Dame is high on the list."

September 26: McLaughlin visits Batton and Werley, and later notes in the prospect's recruiting file that "Dave seems to be interested—good kid, easy to talk to."

September 27: McLaughlin sends follow-up letters to Batton and Werley, thanking them for the opportunity to visit.

October (undated): Werley writes "to inform you that Dave Batton has systematically narrowed his choices to ten schools, including your university, [and] to reiterate our recruiting guidelines. . . . There will be no communication by phone, letter or visit during our season. I will hold all letters for him, and perhaps periodically give them to him, but I will make every effort to keep his mind on academics and Cougar basketball."

October 26: Batton and Werley arrive for the prospect's expense-paid campus visit. Dave watches practice, eats dinner with the team, and attends a pep rally for the Southern Cal football game.

October 27: Batton eats breakfast with McLaughlin, and is later interviewed by the director of admissions and the academic advisor. This afternoon, he joins two other visiting prospects on the fifty-yard line.

October 29: As a follow-up to the visit, Phelps writes to Batton, in care of Werley: "I am sure that if you set your values high in life, the University of Notre Dame can give you everything that you are striving for. I certainly hope that you put all colleges out of your mind during the season. It is important to your coach as well as your team. . . . We will be in the background all winter, and I want you to understand that we definitely would love to have you with us as a member of the Notre Dame family." Phelps comments in a letter to Werley, "You could let me borrow your sport jacket. I am sure that it would look very nice on national TV." Finally, Phelps puts this assessment in the recruiting file: "Dave is a great kid . . . college boards should be better . . . he is sold on Notre Dame academically and athletically."

November 5: Phelps visits Batton and his parents in Springfield. He notes later: "I'm sure they will let Dave make his own decision. . . . Skip told me that Villanova, Kentucky and Notre Dame are his top three choices. Yet Skip felt that Maryland could get in the picture before it's over. . . . On their return trip from South Bend, Skip and Dave discussed the advantage of being independent as compared to the pressure of a conference school. We have to keep selling this point."

November 6: Phelps sends follow-up letters to Batton and Werley. He says to Batton, "I certainly hope you make it to the state finals." He tells the coach, "I am thoroughly convinced that Dave is just a great kid who has a tremendous future ahead of him."

November 13: Continuing the informal contact, Phelps writes to Batton again: "I would like to take this opportunity to wish you the best of luck in your final high school cage season. . . . We urge you to continue to prepare yourself in the classroom. . . . We are planning to see several of your games. . . . I hope you will be following the Notre Dame team."

November 26: Time for another letter. "Our goal is to make sure that players are successful not only in basketball but in life," Digger writes to the prospect. "We are interested in the complete development of our student-athletes."

December 19: "Merry Christmas and Happy New Year."

January 22, 1974: DiBiaso asks Batton's high school guidance counselor to update his academic standing.

January 31: After watching Batton play, DiBiaso reports that he "does well in warm-up—jumps high, shoots outside 'J'—scores, but doesn't dominate defensively. Doubt if he would be ready as a frosh, but very good potential. . . . Told Dave afterwards that his personal statement [on why he wants to attend Notre Dame] is all that is needed to complete his application."

February 5: McLaughlin and Phelps watch Batton play, and Frank concludes that he "moves well, passes well, shoots well."

February 8: Phelps writes to Batton: "I feel that you could help us in your first year, yet as I told your mother, there would be no pressure on you, since you would have upperclassmen to help you make the adjustment to college basketball." He writes to Dave's parents: "Now that Dave is in his final semester, you no doubt are giving serious consideration to his academic and athletic future. . . . There is no question that Dave would be a valuable asset to our university and would help us as we strive for all-around excellence." Enclosed with the letter is a packet of newspaper clippings extolling the school and this season's basketball success. Finally, he writes to Werley: "I was really impressed with your style of play the other night in Philadelphia."

March 18: With the Springfield and Notre Dame seasons both over, the final recruiting push begins. DiBiaso calls Werley to set up an appointment, but he is shocked to hear that the Irish are no longer being considered. According to Werley, Dave fears that Notre Dame has too much undergraduate talent, and he believes that the Irish coaches showed too *little* interest in him during the season. His choices have narrowed to Villanova, Kentucky and, sure enough, Maryland.

Despite this disheartening development, DiBiaso advises Phelps, "I think we still have a chance." McLaughlin is even more confident. "He can be gotten if we tell him we spend more time with the players we already have than the ones we're trying to recruit."

Phelps persists in the fight by calling Werley. "Dave is the big kid we want," he emphasizes. "With Shumate possibly leaving, he should come in with the attitude that he can win a position."

Werley agrees that Notre Dame may have been excluded prematurely. He offers to discuss the matter with Batton and promises to get back in touch.

March 20–21: Werley has not been heard from, so McLaughlin hurries to Pennsylvania to speak with the recruit personally. Frank finds Batton's response to his overtures encouraging, and he assesses the situation this way: "His two big questions are: Can he play? And can he do the school work? . . . We must spend time with him and make him believe in us. . . . We should get him if we work."

March 26: Batton receives a telegram from "Digger Phelps and the Notre Dame family" which reads, "Best wishes on your 18th birthday. Hope you can celebrate your 19th birthday in San Diego with a national championship."

March 27: After Phelps and McLaughlin visit the Batton family in Springfield, McLaughlin reports that "things look good."

March 28–31: McLaughlin, in Pittsburgh for the Dapper Dan games, "spends a lot of time with Dave."

April 1: Now sensing a definite change in Batton's attitude, McLaughlin writes to the Battons: "We feel that we can offer him a combination of an outstanding education, and an opportunity to play in one of the finest programs in the country."

April 3: Aware that Batton was visited yesterday by Kentucky, McLaughlin bears down on his quarry. He returns to Springfield and jokes, "Dave, all of these trips are ruining my love life, but I'm not leaving until you tell me you will come to Notre Dame."

April 4: Batton tells McLaughlin he will come to Notre Dame. McLaughlin quickly relays the good news to Phelps, who writes to assistant admissions director Myron Busby: "Last September, our staff screened the top 15 big men in the country and we immediately ruled out 12 because of academic deficiencies. [Of those remaining] Mark Olberding chose to attend Minnesota, [and] we decided Rick Robey would not fit our style of play. . . . Now the only big man who qualifies is Dave Batton. . . . Dave has indicated that if he is accepted, he would love to attend Notre Dame. There is no doubt that Dave would be a great asset to our basketball program, and I strongly feel that Dave will be a great credit to the university as a student-athlete. Therefore, I would greatly appreciate all the consideration that may be given Dave concerning his acceptance."

April 5: Phelps flies to Pennsylvania and signs Batton to a preliminary scholarship agreement with Notre Dame.

April 17: Told that Batton will be accepted, McLaughlin returns to Pennsylvania to sign him to the national letter-of-intent. Frank also introduces Dave to Leonard Tose, an Irish alumus who owns the Philadelphia Eagles. Tose gives Dave a summer job.

\* \* \*

Winning and successful recruiting are synonymous in college basketball. The coaches who recruit best are the most successful. Those who are either unable or unwilling never get very far or last very long.

No more than fifty schools recruit seriously enough to compete for the national championship. Fewer than that have coaches who can win it. A good coach will struggle if he is not a good recruiter. A good recruiter will be successful, even if he is not a good coach. When both those qualities exist in the same man—or on the same staff—the result is success. More often than not, the frustration of trying to recruit is what causes coaches to quit or move on to other jobs, and not simply the disappointment of losing.

Successful recruiting means finding the players, maintaining contact with them, talking to their parents and coaches, arranging summer jobs, selling yourself, and selling your school. You never know what will influence a prospect the most or turn him off the fastest. But only a phony would say his school is "the best."

For some schools recruiting unfortunately includes cheating or sacrificing academic principles. I favor the strongest rules and the strictest enforcement possible. I fully endorse a rule passed at the 1974 NCAA convention which makes an illegally recruited player ineligible for postseason tournaments. If the rule had been in effect in recent years, Florida State would not have reached the NCAA finals in 1972, and North Carolina State would not have won the championship in 1974.

I would like to see the rules made even stronger. Parents should have to sign a letter spelling out what the NCAA permits their sons to receive. During a guilty school's probationary period, it should be not only ineligible for the tournament, but also ineligible for ranking and Coach of the Year awards. The player involved should be given the choice of transferring to another school or continuing his education in a nonplaying role. He should never play for the school which illegally recruited him. There were ten major college and college-division schools on probation this year, almost all for recruiting violations.

Many schools aren't committed to recruiting because it's an expensive undertaking. We spend about $15,000 a year for recruiting trips, and I know of schools which spend as much as $70,000 and conferences which average $35,000 per team. When Adrian Dantley delayed his decision until the middle of June last year, my extra travel to and from Washington actually put us over our budget. I've since decided that the recruiting season should end no later than May 30. This is well beyond the national letter-of-intent day (April 17), so it seems like a reasonable deadline. The problem is caused by the increasing number of weekend all-star games which can delay the prospects' campus visits.

Being recruited is an ego trip for many kids. They enjoy the travel, the attention, and the competition among schools. They sit in their homes and watch the fifty best-dressed men in America parade through their living rooms.

For coaches, it's the most difficult and frustrating part of the business. What does his mother think? What does his father think? Who else is the player talking to? Can I talk to him last? What if the weather is bad on his visit? When recruiting intensifies in the first few weeks after the playing season, a coach must forget his family, his golf game, and his sensibility.

We never sign all the players we would like to have. Some years are better than others. Occasionally we make serious mistakes in judgment. In 1972, I thought Mitch Kupchak of North Carolina would not help us as much as some other prospects we were going after. I was wrong.

There's no such thing as a hidden talent these days. High school scouting services and word-of-mouth let any coach know who the good players are. However, I don't keep up with this nearly so carefully as Dick and

Frank, who handle the paper work and preliminary evaluations.

Most of the five hundred players we consider every year are quickly eliminated on the basis of grades, or our judgment that they are unsuited for either major-college basketball or our particular program. We see the rest either on film or in person. After watching fifteen or twenty players a year, we pick about ten to concentrate on. If we sign three or four from our "blue chip" list, we feel we've done a good job.

The good players can be found everywhere today. Three of the best areas are New York, Washington, and Southern California. Some states, like Texas and Florida, suffer from lack of interest. Most of the athletes in Texas want to play football, and everyone in Florida wants to go to the beach.

We look for students with sound high school coaching who played against top-notch competition. We like them to know how to win and be receptive to hard work and instruction.

And finally, we want players who believe in what Notre Dame has to offer: the traditions, the education, the athletic excellence. We recruit by selling these advantages, not by knocking the competition.

# RECORDS APPENDIX

* 1973–74 Roster
* 1973–74 Statistics
* 1973–74 Results
* Final Associated Press Top 20
* Postseason Honors

## 1973–74 Roster

| NO. | NAME | POS. | HT. | WT. | ELIG. | HOMETOWN | HIGH SCHOOL | COACH |
|-----|------|------|-----|-----|-------|----------|-------------|-------|
| 54 | Anderson, Roger | F-C | 6-9 | 220 | So. | St. Paul, Minn. | St. Thomas Academy | Terry Flynn |
| 25 | Brokaw, Gary | G | 6-3 | 175 | Jr. | New Brunswick, N.J. | New Brunswick | Bob Burnstein |
| 15 | Clay, Dwight | G | 6-0 | 170 | Jr. | Pittsburgh, Pa. | Fifth Avenue | Elmer Guckert |
| 40 | Crotty, Peter | F | 6-8 | 190 | Jr. | Rockville Centre, N.Y. | St. Agnes | Frank Morriss |
| 44 | Dantley, Adrian | F | 6-5 | 225 | Fr. | Washington, D.C. | DeMatha | Morgan Wootten |
| 31 | Drew, Bill | G | 6-5 | 185 | Fr. | Commack, N.Y. | Centereach | Michael Browne |
| 22 | Hansen, Tom | G | 6-2 | 175 | Sr. | Erie, Pa. | Cathedral Prep | Richard Fox |
| 43 | Knight, Toby | F-C | 6-9 | 198 | Fr. | Port Jefferson, N.Y. | Vandermeulin | Don Frisina |
| 23 | Kuzmicz, Dave | G | 6-3 | 185 | Fr. | South Bend, Ind. | St. Joseph's | Bob Donewald |
| 21 | Martin, Ray | G | 6-1 | 168 | Fr. | Long Island City, N.Y. | Mater Christi | Jim Gatto |
| 35 | Novak, Gary | F | 6-7 | 195 | Sr. | LaSalle, Ill. | LaSalle-Peru | Jim Margenthaler |
| 55 | Paterno, Bill | F | 6-5 | 200 | Fr. | Lincroft, N.J. | Christian Brothers | Vinnie Cox |
| 42 | Schmelzer, Greg | F | 6-6 | 205 | Sr. | Park Ridge, Ill. | Maine South | Bernard Brady |
| 51 | Schuckman, Myron | F-C | 6-9 | 210 | So. | McCracken, Kan. | McCracken | Glenn Conner |
| 34 | Shumate, John | C | 6-9 | 235 | Jr. | Elizabeth, N.J. | Thomas Jefferson | Ron Kelly |
| 41 | Stevens, Chris | F | 6-6 | 200 | Sr. | Washington, D.C. | St. John's Academy | Joe Gallagher |
| 24 | Varga, Tom | G | 5-11 | 170 | Jr. | South Bend, Ind. | St. Joseph's | Bob Donewald |
| 33 | Wolbeck, Ken | F | 6-7 | 205 | Sr. | Peoria, Ill. | Spaulding | Ron Patterson |

*Coach: Digger Phelps (Rider '63)*
*Assistants: Dick DiBiaso (Mansfield State '62), Frank McLaughlin (Fordham '69)*

## 1973–74 Statistics

| PLAYER | G | TIME | FGM-FGA | PCT. | FTM-FTA | PCT. | REB | AVG. | PF-FO | A | TP | AVG. |
|---|---|---|---|---|---|---|---|---|---|---|---|---|
| Shumate | 29 | 1029 | 281–448 | .627 | 141–196 | .719 | 319 | 11.0 | 65 | 56 | 703 | 24.2 |
| Dantley | 28 | 795 | 189–339 | .558 | 133–161 | .826 | 255 | 9.7 | 74–2 | 40 | 511 | 18.3 |
| Brokaw | 28 | 962 | 201–361 | .557 | 76–109 | .697 | 124 | 4.4 | 73–2 | 104 | 478 | 17.1 |
| Paterno | 29 | 566 | 95–190 | .500 | 33–46 | .717 | 99 | 3.4 | 59–3 | 18 | 223 | 7.7 |
| Novak | 29 | 728 | 97–186 | .522 | 16–39 | .410 | 174 | 6.0 | 49 | 68 | 210 | 7.2 |
| Clay | 28 | 817 | 89–223 | .399 | 23–29 | .793 | 61 | 2.2 | 47 | 136 | 201 | 7.2 |
| Martin | 27 | 439 | 32–68 | .471 | 22–35 | .628 | 30 | 1.1 | 42 | 58 | 86 | 3.2 |
| Knight | 18 | 87 | 18–38 | .474 | 12–15 | .800 | 37 | 2.1 | 18 | 5 | 48 | 2.7 |
| Crotty | 22 | 132 | 10–32 | .313 | 18–25 | .720 | 33 | 1.5 | 19 | 11 | 38 | 1.7 |
| Drew | 13 | 65 | 15–31 | .484 | 4–7 | .571 | 10 | 0.8 | 3 | 1 | 34 | 2.8 |
| Kuzmicz | 18 | 79 | 9–28 | .321 | 11–16 | .688 | 10 | 0.6 | 14 | 5 | 29 | 1.6 |
| Stevens | 9 | 19 | 6–12 | .500 | 0–1 | .000 | 5 | 0.5 | 3 | 2 | 12 | 1.3 |
| Anderson | 10 | 23 | 3–9 | .333 | 3–6 | .500 | 8 | 0.7 | 1 | 2 | 9 | 0.9 |
| Schuckman | 13 | 32 | 3–6 | .500 | 2–4 | .500 | 7 | 0.5 | 4 | 1 | 8 | 0.6 |
| Schmelzer | 9 | 16 | 4–13 | .308 | 0–0 | .000 | 6 | 0.6 | 4 | 1 | 8 | 0.8 |
| Wolbeck | 2 | 4 | 2–5 | .400 | 0–0 | .000 | 0 | 0.0 | 0 | 0 | 4 | 2.0 |
| Varga | 2 | 4 | 2–3 | .666 | 0–0 | .000 | 0 | 0.0 | 0 | 0 | 4 | 2.0 |
| Hansen | 1 | 3 | 0–0 | .000 | 0–0 | .000 | 1 | 1.0 | 1 | 0 | 0 | 0.0 |
| Team | | | | | | | 162 | | | | | |
| Notre Dame | 29 | | 1056–1992 | .530 | 494–689 | .717 | 1341 | 46.2 | 470–7 | 506 | 2606 | 89.9 |
| Opponents | 29 | | 933–2092 | .446 | 250–373 | .670 | 1071 | 36.9 | 518–27 | 321 | 2116 | 73.0 |

## 1973–74 Results

| RESULTS ND | OPP | | ATTN. | SCORING LEADERS | | | REBOUNDS | |
|---|---|---|---|---|---|---|---|---|
| + 112 | 62 | Valparaiso-H | 11,063 | Dantley 16, | Shumate | 15 | Dantley | 9 |
| + 76 ot | 72 | Ohio State-A | 13,279c | Shumate 25, | Brokaw | 15 | Shumate | 17 |
| + 98 | 74 | Northwestern-A | 5,671 | Shumate 30, | Brokaw | 22 | Dantley | 9 |
| + 94 | 65 | St. Louis-H | 11,156 | Shumate 19, | Brokaw | 18 | Dantley | 8 |
| + 73 | 67 | Indiana-A | 17,463c | Shumate 26, | Paterno | 16 | Shumate | 15 |
| + 99 | 59 | Denver-H | 10,463 | Dantley 21, | Shumate | 16 | Dantley | 8 |
| + 94 | 79 | Kentucky-A | 16,613c | Shumate 25, | Dant-Brok | 22 | Shumate | 14 |
| + 87 | 44 | Xavier-H | 10,117 | Shumate 19, | Brokaw | 14 | Shumate | 10 |
| + 104 | 77 | Georgetown-H | 11,160 | Shumate 26, | Dantley | 22 | Dantley | 10 |
| + 71 | 70 | UCLA-H | 11,345c | Brokaw 25, | Shumate | 24 | Shumate | 11 |
| + 76 | 74 | Kansas-A | 17,100c | Shumate 23, | Dantley | 17 | Dantley | 8 |
| + 78 | 58 | St. Francis-H | 11,345c | Dantley 22, | Shumate | 19 | Shu-Dant | 11 |
| − 74 | 94 | UCLA-A | 12,874c | Shumate 25, | Brokaw | 14 | Brokaw | 6 |
| + 69 | 63 | Marquette-H | 11,345c | Shumate 27, | Paterno | 14 | Novak | 6 |
| + 101 | 72 | DePaul-H | 11,068 | Brokaw 25, | Dantley | 23 | Dantley | 15 |
| + 95 | 84 | Davidson-H | 11,345c | Shumate 25, | Brokaw | 24 | Shumate | 14 |
| + 91 | 89 | Michigan St.-A | 12,500c | Shumate 27, | Brokaw | 21 | Dantley | 9 |
| + 98 | 78 | LaSalle-A | 9,222c | Brokaw 28, | Shumate | 24 | Novak | 10 |
| + 87 | 68 | Duke-H | 11,345c | Dantley 27, | Shumate | 25 | Dantley | 15 |
| + 79 | 69 | Fordham-A | 14,682 | Dantley 27, | Shumate | 16 | Shumate | 10 |
| + 72 | 68 | South Carolina-A | 12,576c | Shumate 26, | Dantley | 17 | Brokaw | 15 |
| + 85 | 68 | Western Michigan-H | 11,345c | Shumate 26, | Dantley | 23 | Shumate | 14 |
| + 108 | 80 | West Virginia-H | 11,345c | Dantley 41, | Shumate | 25 | Shumate | 13 |
| + 93 | 69 | Ball State-H | 11,345c | Shumate 31, | Dantley | 26 | Shumate | 15 |
| + 115 | 85 | Villanova-H | 11,345c | Brokaw 26, | Shumate | 24 | Shumate | 16 |
| − 82 | 97 | Dayton-A | 13,528c | Shumate 29, | Brokaw | 13 | Shumate | 16 |
| + 108 | 66 | Austin Peay-NCAA | 10,100c | Brokaw 25, | Shu-Dant | 22 | Shu-Dant | 10 |
| − 68 | 77 | Michigan-NCAA | 15,014c | Shumate 34, | Novak | 11 | Shumate | 17 |
| + 118 | 88 | Vanderbilt-NCAA | 15,014c | Shumate 30, | Dantley | 29 | Dantley | 10 |

## Single-Game Highs

Points–118 v. Vanderbilt           Dantley (41)
v. W. Virginia

Field Goals–50 v. Austin Peay       Dantley (18)
v. W. Virginia

Field Goals Attempted–87 v. Valpo & W. Va.    Dantley (23)
v. W. Virginia

Field-Goal Percentage–.629 v. Michigan St.    Novak (5–5, 1.000)
v. Michigan St.

Free Throws–26 v. LaSalle         Dantley (12)
v. Georgetown

Free-Throw Percent–.952 v. Vanderbilt    Dantley (11–11, 1.000)
v. So. Carolina

Rebounds–68 v. Xavier           Shumate (17)
v. Ohio St., Michigan

Assists–31 v. Valparaiso          Brokaw (10)
v. W. Virginia


## Final Associated Press Top 20

| | | | | |
|---|---|---|---|---|
| 1. | N.C. State | 30–1 | .968 | NCAA champion |
| 2. | UCLA | 26–4 | .867 | NCAA third place |
| 3. | Marquette | 26–5 | .839 | NCAA runner-up |
| 4. | Maryland | 23–5 | .821 | ACC tournament runner-up |
| 5. | Notre Dame | 26–3 | .897 | Mideast third place |
| 6. | Michigan | 22–5 | .815 | Mideast runner-up |
| 7. | Kansas | 23–7 | .767 | NCAA fourth place |
| 8. | Providence | 28–4 | .875 | East third place |
| 9. | Indiana | 23–5 | .821 | CCT champion |
| 10. | Long Beach State | 23–2 | .920 | Probation |
| 11. | Purdue | 21–9 | .700 | NIT champion |
| 12. | North Carolina | 22–6 | .786 | Eliminated in NIT |
| 13. | Vanderbilt | 23–5 | .821 | Mideast fourth place |
| 14. | Alabama | 22–4 | .846 | SEC runner-up |
| 15. | Utah | 22–8 | .733 | NIT runner-up |
| 16. | Pittsburgh | 25–4 | .862 | East runner-up |
| 17. | Southern California | 24–5 | .828 | CCT runner-up |
| 18. | Oral Roberts | 23–5 | .821 | Midwest runner-up |
| 19. | South Carolina | 22–5 | .815 | Eliminated, first round of Eastern Reg. |
| 20. | Dayton | 20–9 | .690 | West fourth place |

# Postseason Honors

**Digger Phelps**
Coach of the Year by United Press International, *Basketball Weekly, The Sporting News,* Metropolitan Basketball Writers of New York; District IV Coach of the Year by National Association of College Basketball Coaches.

**John Shumate**
Notre Dame Most Valuable Player
Notre Dame Field Goal Award
Consensus All-American (AP, UPI, NACBC, *Basketball Weekly,* Helms, NBA)
Member of Pizza Hut Classic East All-Star Team
Drafted by Phoenix of NBA (and by Virginia of ABA in 1973)

**Gary Brokaw**
Most Improved Notre Dame Player
Third Team All-American by UPI
All-District IV by NACBC
All-Midwest by *Basketball Weekly*
Outstanding Visiting Player by Philadelphia Basketball Writers
Drafted by Milwaukee of NBA and New York of ABA

**Gary Novak**
Notre Dame Outstanding Defensive Player
Academic All-American
Member of Pizza Hut Classic East All-Star Team
NCAA Postgraduate Scholarship Winner
Drafted by Cleveland of NBA and Carolina of ABA

**Adrian Dantley**
Notre Dame Free-Throw Award
Freshman All-American by *Basketball Weekly*
Honorable Mention All-American by UPI, AP
Outstanding Visiting Player by Metropolitan Basketball Writers of New York

**Dwight Clay**
Notre Dame Outstanding Play-Maker

**Monogram Winners**
John Shumate, Gary Brokaw, Gary Novak, Adrian Dantley, Dwight Clay, Peter Crotty, Bill Paterno, Ray Martin, Toby Knight, Dave Kuzmicz, Bill Drew